Detoxing adrenaline Workbook

by

Steven Morken

Front Matter

This book is dedicated to the resilient spirits who carry the weight of unspoken burdens, to those who navigate the complexities of trauma with quiet strength, and to those who seek solace and healing in the depths of their own being. It is a testament to the enduring power of the human spirit, the capacity for self-compassion, and the unwavering belief in the possibility of a life lived with greater peace and joy. It is dedicated to the unsung heroes who fight their battles unseen, and who find the strength to embrace the journey towards wholeness. May these pages serve as a gentle companion on your path, offering a space for self-discovery, understanding, and ultimately, liberation. This work is also dedicated to the countless individuals who have shared their stories, experiences, and wisdom, illuminating the path for others to follow. Their courage and vulnerability have inspired this book and are at its very heart.

The journey to healing from prolonged stress and trauma is rarely linear. It is a winding path, often marked by setbacks and breakthroughs, moments of intense clarity and periods of quiet reflection. This workbook recognizes and honors the complexity of this journey. It offers not a quick fix, but a compassionate and self-guided approach to reclaiming your well-being. Within these pages, you will find tools and techniques rooted in mindfulness and somatic practices, designed to gently nurture your body and mind. This is not a race against time, but a conscious invitation to slow down, to listen deeply to your inner wisdom, and to approach your healing process with the same kindness and understanding you would offer a cherished friend. Remember that progress, no matter how small, is progress. Celebrate the victories, acknowledge the challenges, and embrace the ongoing process of self-discovery with self-compassion and unwavering self-belief. This workbook is a companion, a guide, a safe space to explore your experiences, and ultimately, a tool to foster resilience and build a future filled with greater peace and joy. Your strength and courage are your greatest allies on this journey. Believe in your ability to heal, to grow, and to thrive.

This workbook provides a practical framework for understanding and managing the effects of prolonged stress and trauma. It acknowledges the profound impact that living in a state of constant hypervigilance can have on your physical, emotional, and mental well-being. The constant activation of your "fight-or-flight" response, driven by adrenaline and a heightened sense of threat, takes a significant toll. This book recognizes that true healing is not about erasing painful experiences but about learning to integrate them into your life narrative in a way that doesn't dictate your future. The approach offered here emphasizes building emotional resilience, not through forced positivity or denial of difficult emotions, but through a compassionate and grounded approach to self-discovery. We will explore techniques to gently soothe your nervous system, to re-regulate your emotional responses, and to cultivate a sense of inner peace. The tools and exercises included are designed to be adaptable to your individual needs and pace. This isn't a rigid program, but an invitation to engage with the material in a way that feels supportive and empowering. Journaling prompts, guided meditations, and somatic practices will be interwoven throughout, encouraging you to connect with your inner wisdom and build a deeper understanding of your unique experiences. Remember that your healing is a deeply personal journey, and there is no right or wrong way to navigate this process. Allow yourself the space to move at your own pace, honoring your own timeline. With patience, self-compassion, and a willingness to explore your inner landscape, you can cultivate greater resilience and build a more fulfilling and peaceful life.

Chapter 1: Understanding Your Stress Response

Our bodies are incredibly sophisticated systems, constantly adapting and responding to the world around us. This adaptability is crucial for survival, allowing us to react quickly to threats and navigate challenges. However, when faced with prolonged stress or trauma, this finely tuned system can become overloaded, leading to a cascade of physiological changes that impact our physical and mental well-being. Understanding these biological mechanisms is crucial to understanding why we react the way we do and to developing effective strategies for healing.

Let's begin by exploring the key players in our stress response: the amygdala, the hippocampus, and the prefrontal cortex. Think of your brain as a complex computer, with these three areas acting as crucial processing units. The amygdala, often described as the brain's "emotional center," is our early warning system. It's constantly scanning for potential threats, both real and perceived. When it detects a threat—a loud noise, a looming deadline, a memory of past trauma—it triggers the "fight-or-flight" response. This involves the release of stress hormones like cortisol and adrenaline, preparing the body for action. Your heart rate increases, your breathing quickens, and your muscles tense—all designed to help you either confront the threat or escape from it.

The hippocampus, on the other hand, plays a critical role in memory formation and retrieval. It's responsible for contextualizing experiences, helping us understand the "where" and "when" of events. In stressful situations, the hippocampus works alongside the amygdala to encode the details of the threat. This is why traumatic events are often vividly remembered, sometimes even in excruciating detail. However, prolonged or extreme stress can impair the hippocampus's function, leading to memory problems, difficulty with recall, and even the distortion of memories.

The prefrontal cortex, the brain's executive control center, is responsible for higher-level cognitive functions like planning, decision-making, and emotional regulation. It acts as a moderator, tempering the amygdala's alarm signals and helping us respond in a more rational and adaptive way. Imagine it as the "cool-headed" part of your brain, trying to keep the "panicked" amygdala in check. However, when constantly bombarded by stress, the prefrontal cortex can become overwhelmed, leading to impaired judgment, difficulty concentrating, and an increased susceptibility to emotional reactivity.

This interplay between the amygdala, hippocampus, and prefrontal cortex is crucial in understanding the physiological effects of prolonged stress and trauma. Chronic stress can lead to an overactive amygdala, constantly perceiving threats even when none exist. This can manifest as hypervigilance, anxiety, and an increased sensitivity to environmental cues. Simultaneously, a stressed hippocampus may struggle to process information accurately, leading to distorted memories and difficulty forming new ones. A chronically overloaded prefrontal cortex loses its capacity for rational decision-making and emotional regulation, leading to impulsive behaviors, difficulty concentrating, and heightened emotional reactivity.

Consider the impact of a single traumatic event, such as a car accident. The amygdala immediately registers the danger, triggering a surge of adrenaline and cortisol. The hippocampus encodes the terrifying sensory details: the screech of tires, the impact, the feeling of fear. The prefrontal cortex tries to make sense of the situation, but the intensity of the experience might temporarily overwhelm its ability to regulate the emotional response. The immediate aftermath might see heightened anxiety, intrusive thoughts, and difficulty sleeping.

However, the effects of trauma don't end with the acute phase. The body's stress response remains activated long after the event itself. This constant state of hyperarousal can lead to numerous physical and mental health problems. Chronic stress can impact nearly every system in the body. It can disrupt sleep cycles, weaken the immune system, increase the risk of cardiovascular disease, and contribute to digestive problems. Mentally, it can lead to anxiety disorders, depression, post-traumatic stress disorder (PTSD), and other mental health challenges. The prolonged activation of the stress response also impacts the hypothalamic-pituitary-adrenal (HPA) axis, a complex system that regulates stress hormones. Over time, the HPA axis can become dysregulated, leading to an imbalance in hormone levels and a heightened vulnerability to stress.

Imagine the HPA axis as a thermostat that regulates your body's response to stress. In a healthy state, this thermostat is finely tuned, responding appropriately to stressors and then returning to baseline once the threat is gone. However, chronic stress can damage this thermostat, causing it to malfunction. This can result in an overproduction of stress hormones, even in the absence of a true threat. This chronic elevation of cortisol, for example, can lead to a range of health problems, including weight gain, impaired immune function, and an increased risk of heart disease.

The impact of chronic stress on the brain is also profound. Studies show that prolonged exposure to stress hormones can actually shrink the hippocampus, reducing its ability to form and retrieve memories effectively. Conversely, the amygdala, already hyperactive from chronic stress, may become even more sensitive to threats. This vicious cycle fuels anxiety and fear, perpetuating the cycle of stress and trauma.

Moreover, the effects of stress and trauma aren't always immediately obvious. The symptoms can be subtle and insidious, manifesting as persistent fatigue, difficulty concentrating, irritability, or changes in sleep patterns. These symptoms can easily be mistaken for other conditions, delaying proper diagnosis and treatment. It's crucial to remember that the experience of stress and trauma is highly individual, and there's no single "right" way to respond. Some individuals might exhibit outward signs of distress, while others may internalize their experiences, showing few outward signs of struggle. This variability highlights the importance of self-awareness and seeking professional help when needed.

Understanding the physiological underpinnings of stress and trauma is not about pathologizing or labeling individuals. Instead, it's about developing a deeper understanding of the body's complex response to adversity. This knowledge can equip us with the tools to create a more compassionate and effective approach to healing, enabling us to work with our bodies, not against them, as we navigate the path to recovery. By understanding how our brains and bodies react to stress, we can begin to develop strategies to regulate our nervous systems, reframe our narratives, and ultimately, create a more peaceful and resilient future for ourselves. The path to healing is rarely straightforward, and it requires patience, self-compassion, and a willingness to engage with both the mental and physical aspects of our well-being. The following chapters will provide practical tools and techniques to support this journey, guiding you on a path of self-discovery and empowerment.

Our previous exploration of the physiological stress response provides a foundational understanding of *why* we react as we do to challenging circumstances. Now, let's turn our attention to *what* specifically triggers those reactions within your individual experience. Identifying your personal stressors is a crucial first step in managing your stress response and fostering resilience. This isn't about blame or self-criticism; rather, it's about gaining a clearer picture of your unique landscape of challenges.

Think of your life as a tapestry woven with many threads. Some threads are vibrant and joyful, representing positive experiences and fulfilling relationships. Others are darker and more frayed, representing challenges, losses, and ongoing difficulties. These frayed threads often represent the stressors that contribute to your feeling of constant hypervigilance, that sense of being perpetually "on guard."

Pinpointing these stressors requires introspection and honest self-reflection. It's a journey of self-discovery, and like any journey, it might feel uncomfortable at times. However, the clarity you gain will be invaluable in your path to healing. A useful tool in this process is journaling. Take some time each day, even just five or ten minutes, to write down your thoughts and feelings. Don't worry about grammar or style; simply let your thoughts flow onto the page.

One effective journaling prompt is to ask yourself: "What situations, people, or thoughts consistently leave me feeling overwhelmed, anxious, or on edge?" Pay attention to the recurring patterns in your responses. Do you find yourself feeling particularly stressed around deadlines at work? Do arguments with loved ones leave you feeling drained and emotionally exhausted? Do specific memories trigger intense physical or emotional reactions? These are all potential areas to investigate further.

Let's consider stressors across various life domains. In the professional sphere, demanding workloads, unreasonable deadlines, workplace conflict, or lack of control over your work environment can be significant contributors to stress. Consider the specifics: is it the volume of work, the lack of support from colleagues, or the pressure to constantly perform? The precise nature of the stressor can significantly inform your approach to mitigating its impact.

Similarly, your personal relationships can be a source of both joy and stress. Strained relationships with family members, conflicts with partners or friends, or the feeling of emotional isolation can all significantly impact your well-being. Examine the dynamics of your relationships: are there consistent patterns of conflict? Do you feel heard and understood? Do you feel supported emotionally? Understanding the source of the stress within your relationships is crucial to navigating them constructively.

Your physical health is another critical area to consider. Chronic pain, illnesses, or lack of physical activity can all contribute to feelings of stress and overwhelm. Even seemingly minor physical discomfort, if persistent, can disrupt your daily routines and increase your levels of anxiety. Notice any physical sensations that accompany feelings of stress: tension in your shoulders, tightness in your chest, stomach upset. These physical manifestations can be valuable clues to the underlying stressors.

Financial difficulties also frequently rank as major stressors. The worry of making ends meet, managing debt, or unexpected financial setbacks can significantly impact mental and emotional well-being. This stress is often pervasive, permeating other aspects of your life. Recognizing the financial pressures you are under is crucial to finding solutions or seeking support.

Consider the impact of your social environment. Living in a high-crime area, facing discrimination, or lacking a strong social support network can all contribute to chronic stress. Isolation and loneliness can amplify feelings of anxiety and vulnerability. Are there aspects of your social environment that leave you feeling unsafe or unsupported?

Even seemingly minor daily annoyances, when they accumulate over time, can contribute significantly to your overall stress load. Traffic jams, long lines at the grocery store, constant interruptions, these seemingly insignificant events can become significant triggers when combined with larger stressors. These "micro-stressors" are often overlooked, yet their cumulative effect can be substantial.

To gain a clearer understanding of your stressors, consider using a simple categorization exercise. Create a list of your stressors and then categorize them by two criteria: impact and frequency. Impact refers to how significantly each stressor affects your well-being. Frequency refers to how often you experience each stressor. Using a scale of 1 to 5 (1 being low and 5 being high) for both impact and frequency, rate each stressor on both scales. This will help you visualize which stressors are most impactful and prevalent in your life. You might be surprised to discover that seemingly minor daily annoyances, when experienced frequently, have a surprisingly high cumulative impact on your stress levels.

For example, let's say you consistently feel overwhelmed by work deadlines (high impact, high frequency), experience occasional conflicts with family members (medium impact, low frequency), and regularly struggle with traffic congestion during your commute (low impact, high frequency). This exercise helps you prioritize which stressors to address first, focusing on those with high impact and high frequency. It provides a visual representation of your stress landscape, offering a roadmap for effective management strategies.

Remember, this process is not about judging yourself or dwelling on negativity. It's about gaining self-awareness, a critical component in navigating the path to healing and building resilience. By identifying your personal stressors, you are taking an active role in managing your well-being and reclaiming your future. The following chapters will provide you with techniques and tools to actively address these identified stressors, fostering a sense of peace and empowering you to navigate your life with greater ease and control. Embrace this process of self-discovery with patience and self-compassion, remembering that healing is a journey, not a destination. Every step forward, no matter how small, is a testament to your strength and resilience.

We've explored the complexities of your stress response and undertaken the crucial step of identifying your personal stressors. This self-awareness is a powerful tool, but it's essential to approach the journey of healing with a realistic understanding of the process itself. A common misconception, one that often fuels frustration and self-criticism, is the belief in linear healing. This myth suggests a straightforward progression, a steady climb towards a final destination of complete recovery. The reality, however, is far more nuanced.

Healing from trauma, stress, or prolonged adversity is rarely, if ever, a straight line. Instead, it's a winding path, characterized by ebbs and flows, periods of significant progress interspersed with plateaus, and even occasional setbacks. Understanding this non-linear nature of healing is paramount to fostering self-compassion and avoiding the pitfalls of unrealistic expectations.

Imagine a mountain climber ascending a challenging peak. They don't ascend steadily and effortlessly to the summit. There are steep inclines, requiring intense effort and focus. There are flat stretches, where progress feels slow or non-existent, despite continued exertion. There might be unexpected slips or falls, necessitating a retreat to regain footing and reassess the route. The climber's journey is a testament to resilience, persistence, and the acceptance of setbacks as an integral part of the ascent. Healing is much the same.

Consider, for instance, the experience of someone recovering from a significant relationship loss. Initially, there may be intense grief, marked by debilitating sadness and a profound sense of emptiness. With time, and through various coping mechanisms, they may begin to experience moments of clarity and even peace. They might start engaging in activities they previously enjoyed, rebuilding their social connections, and fostering a sense of self-worth. However, this progress isn't consistently linear. There will be days, weeks, or even months when the grief resurfaces with renewed intensity, triggering a wave of sadness and despair. This isn't a sign of failure; it's a natural part of the healing process. These setbacks offer opportunities for deeper self-understanding, fostering greater resilience and emotional maturity.

Similarly, someone struggling with post-traumatic stress disorder (PTSD) might experience periods of significant progress in managing their symptoms. Therapy might be helping them process their trauma, mindfulness practices might be reducing their anxiety, and lifestyle changes might be improving their sleep and overall well-being. However, there will likely be times when triggers unexpectedly resurface, leading to flashbacks, nightmares, or intense emotional distress. These episodes, while undeniably painful, are not indicative of a failure to heal. They highlight the enduring impact of trauma and the need for continued self-care and professional support. They are opportunities for learning and growth, for refining coping strategies and strengthening resilience.

The non-linear nature of healing extends beyond individual experiences. Consider the broader context of societal factors influencing well-being. Periods of significant personal growth can be overshadowed by external stressors like economic hardship, political instability, or societal upheaval. These factors can disrupt the healing process, introducing unexpected challenges and requiring a reassessment of coping strategies. This isn't a personal failing; it's a testament to the interconnectedness of our lives and the influence of broader systemic factors on our mental health.

The myth of linear healing often leads to self-criticism and feelings of inadequacy. When progress feels slow or non-existent, or when setbacks occur, individuals might question their ability to heal, leading to feelings of hopelessness and despair. This negative self-talk further undermines the healing process, creating a vicious cycle of self-doubt and discouragement. Replacing this self-critical narrative with self-compassion is crucial. Acknowledge that healing takes time, effort, and resilience. Celebrate small victories, however insignificant they may seem. Learn from setbacks, adapting your strategies as needed.

Remember, healing is not a destination but a process. It's a journey of growth, learning, and self-discovery. It's about building resilience, cultivating self-compassion, and developing a deeper understanding of yourself and your experiences. It's about accepting the complexities of your journey, embracing the ebbs and flows, and recognizing that setbacks are opportunities for growth. Embrace the messiness of the process, knowing that every step, forward or sideways, contributes to your overall progress.

Understanding this non-linearity allows for a more compassionate and realistic approach to your healing journey. Instead of focusing on reaching a utopian state of "perfect" recovery, focus on cultivating emotional regulation skills, strengthening coping mechanisms, and fostering a sense of self-compassion. This is a long-term commitment to your well-being.

To further support this understanding, let's examine some common plateaus and setbacks encountered on the path to healing. A common plateau is the feeling of being stuck. After a period of significant progress, you might find yourself feeling stagnant, unable to move forward. This can be frustrating and disheartening, leading to feelings of hopelessness. It's important to recognize that plateaus are a normal part of the healing process. They often represent a period of integration, where you are consolidating your gains and preparing for the next stage of your journey. During these times, focus on self-care, mindfulness practices, and maintaining a consistent routine

Setbacks, on the other hand, are often unexpected disruptions to your progress. These could manifest as a resurgence of past traumas, the emergence of new stressors, or simply a period of overwhelming emotional distress. Instead of viewing setbacks as failures, view them as opportunities for learning and growth. Reflect on what might have triggered the setback, adjust your coping strategies accordingly, and seek support from loved ones or professionals when needed.

Throughout your journey, remember to cultivate self-compassion. Be kind to yourself, acknowledge your struggles, and celebrate your strengths. Avoid comparing your healing journey to others, recognizing that each individual's path is unique and unfolds at their own pace. There is no "right" way to heal; only your way.

Finally, consider journaling as a valuable tool in documenting your healing journey. Regularly record your thoughts, feelings, and experiences. Note periods of progress, plateaus, and setbacks. Reflect on your coping mechanisms, and identify patterns and triggers. This process of self-reflection will provide valuable insights into your healing journey, fostering a deeper understanding of your strengths, challenges, and overall progress. Your healing journey is a testament to your resilience and your commitment to your well-being. Embrace the process, celebrate your progress, and remember that you are not alone. The path may be winding, but the destination—a life of greater peace, resilience, and well-being—is worth the journey. The following chapters will provide specific strategies and techniques to navigate this journey with greater ease and confidence.

Building a foundation of self-compassion is not merely a helpful addition to your healing journey; it is its bedrock. Without it, the inherent challenges of navigating trauma and stress will likely feel insurmountable, leading to discouragement and hindering progress. Self-compassion, in essence, is the act of treating yourself with the same kindness, understanding, and patience that you would offer a dear friend struggling with similar difficulties. It's recognizing your imperfections, acknowledging your pain, and offering yourself empathy and support rather than harsh judgment and criticism.

This is especially critical in the non-linear landscape of healing. Remember the analogy of the mountain climber? Self-compassion is the climber's internal support system, the unwavering belief in their ability to persevere even when faced with setbacks. It's the voice that whispers encouragement during moments of doubt, reminding them of their resilience and strength. Without this internal resource, the inevitable challenges of the ascent – the steep inclines, the plateaus, the unexpected falls – can feel utterly defeating.

Cultivating self-compassion is not an overnight transformation; it is a practice, a mindful choice made repeatedly, day in and day out. It requires actively challenging the ingrained patterns of self-criticism that often accompany trauma and stress. These patterns, often rooted in past experiences and learned behaviors, can feel as familiar and comfortable as an old sweater, even though they are ultimately harmful.

One of the first steps in building self-compassion is identifying and challenging your negative self-talk. Pay attention to the internal dialogue—the voice that judges your mistakes, amplifies your failures, and minimizes your successes. What are the common themes? Do you often label yourself with negative adjectives? Do you engage in self-blame? Do you compare yourself unfavorably to others? Becoming aware of these self-critical patterns is the first step in dismantling them.

Once you've identified these patterns, begin to challenge their validity. Ask yourself: Is this thought truly helpful? Is it based on facts or assumptions? Would I say this to a friend in a similar situation? Often, the self-critical voice operates on distorted perceptions and unrealistic standards. By questioning its validity, you begin to reclaim your power and cultivate a more compassionate perspective.

Mindfulness plays a crucial role in fostering self-compassion. Through mindfulness practices, such as meditation or deep breathing exercises, you learn to observe your thoughts and feelings without judgment. This non-judgmental awareness creates a space for self-acceptance, allowing you to acknowledge your struggles without succumbing to self-criticism. Instead of fighting your emotions, you learn to witness them, acknowledging their presence without letting them define you.

Mindful self-compassion meditations are particularly effective in fostering this sense of self-acceptance. These guided meditations typically involve focusing on a loving-kindness phrase, often a variation of "May I be kind to myself," "May I be patient with myself," or "May I accept myself as I am." Repeating these phrases silently or aloud, focusing on the sensations in your body, and allowing yourself to feel the emotions arising without resistance, can gradually cultivate a sense of inner peace and self-compassion.

Incorporating mindfulness into your daily routine, even for short periods, can significantly impact your ability to respond to challenges with greater self-compassion. Practicing mindfulness while engaging in everyday activities, such as washing dishes or taking a walk, can enhance your awareness of your physical sensations and emotions, strengthening your ability to approach yourself with kindness and understanding in challenging moments.

Another powerful tool for building self-compassion is journaling. Regular journaling provides a safe space to explore your thoughts and feelings without judgment. It allows you to process your experiences, identify patterns of self-criticism, and cultivate a more compassionate inner dialogue.

Consider journaling prompts that directly target self-compassion. For example:

Describe a recent situation where you were critical of yourself. What thoughts and feelings arose? How could you have responded differently?

Write a letter to yourself from the perspective of a compassionate friend. What would they say to you? What kind of support would they offer?

Identify three things you appreciate about yourself. Focus on your strengths, talents, and accomplishments.

Reflect on a time you showed compassion to another person. How did that experience feel? How can you apply that same compassion to yourself?

Regularly reflecting on these prompts allows for a deeper understanding of your self-critical tendencies and facilitates the development of a more compassionate inner narrative. It's a process of self-discovery, allowing you to gradually replace judgment with understanding and self-criticism with self-acceptance.

Beyond mindfulness and journaling, practicing acts of self-care is crucial in nurturing self-compassion. This isn't about indulging in frivolous luxuries; it's about engaging in activities that nourish your mind, body, and spirit. These might include spending time in nature, engaging in creative pursuits, listening to calming music, practicing yoga or other forms of exercise, spending time with loved ones, or pursuing hobbies you enjoy. By consistently prioritizing self-care, you demonstrate to yourself that you are worthy of kindness, respect, and attention.

Furthermore, remember to actively challenge the comparison trap. Social media, in particular, fosters unhealthy comparisons, leading to feelings of inadequacy and self-criticism. Make a conscious effort to limit your exposure to social media or to engage with it mindfully, focusing on positive content and avoiding accounts that trigger negative self-comparisons. Recognize that each individual's healing journey is unique and unfolds at its own pace. There is no competition, and comparing yourself to others is counterproductive to building self-compassion. Celebrate your progress, no matter how small, and focus on your own individual journey.

Finally, self-compassion is not about ignoring your shortcomings or avoiding responsibility. It's about acknowledging your imperfections, accepting your humanness, and treating yourself with kindness and understanding during the process of growth and change. It's about learning from your mistakes without dwelling on them, and celebrating your successes without letting them inflate your ego. It's about creating a balanced and healthy inner relationship with yourself, one that supports and encourages your progress toward well-being. This foundation of self-compassion will ultimately provide the resilience and strength you need to navigate the ongoing journey of healing from trauma and stress, empowering you to move forward with greater confidence and self-assurance. It is a crucial step towards creating a more fulfilling and meaningful life.

Building a foundation of self-compassion, as discussed, is paramount to navigating the challenges of trauma and stress. However, inner resilience is only part of the equation. Healing also necessitates the creation of a safe and supportive external environment. This environment, both physical and emotional, acts as a protective cocoon, allowing you to process your experiences and rebuild your sense of security. Without this external support, the internal work of self-compassion can feel significantly more challenging, akin to trying to build a house on shifting sand.

Creating a safe environment begins with identifying spaces – both physical locations and emotional states – where you feel protected and secure. This might be a quiet corner of your home, a favorite park, or even a specific memory that evokes feelings of peace and calm. The key is to consciously cultivate these spaces, consciously making them sanctuaries free from triggers and stressors. This might involve decluttering a room, creating a calming ambiance with soft lighting and relaxing scents, or simply setting aside dedicated time for solitude and reflection.

Equally crucial is the cultivation of emotional safety. This involves setting boundaries—defining limits to protect your emotional well-being. These boundaries might involve saying "no" to requests that drain your energy or compromise your emotional stability. It might mean limiting contact with individuals who consistently contribute to your stress or trigger painful memories. Defining these boundaries is an act of self-respect and a critical step in creating a space where your emotional needs are prioritized. Learning to say "no" is not selfish; it's self-preservation. It's a powerful assertion of your right to prioritize your well-being.

The process of setting boundaries might feel uncomfortable initially, particularly if you're accustomed to prioritizing the needs of others above your own. You might experience guilt, anxiety, or fear of rejection. It is important to acknowledge these feelings without judgment. Remember the self-compassion practices we've discussed—treat yourself with the same kindness and understanding you would offer a friend in a similar situation. Start small. Begin by setting boundaries in less challenging situations, gradually working your way up to more difficult interactions. Celebrate every successful boundary you set as a step forward in your healing journey.

Beyond setting personal boundaries, actively seeking support from your loved ones is a vital aspect of creating a supportive environment. This involves sharing your experiences and struggles with people you trust—individuals who can offer empathy, understanding, and practical support. Choosing the right individuals is crucial; these should be people who demonstrate patience, respect, and a willingness to listen without judgment. Sharing your experiences can feel incredibly vulnerable, but it's also incredibly powerful. The act of verbalizing your trauma can help to process it and alleviate some of the associated emotional burden.

It's important to remember that not all support systems are created equal. Some individuals might inadvertently minimize your experience, offer unsolicited advice, or express skepticism towards your feelings. These well-intentioned but ultimately unhelpful responses can leave you feeling dismissed and invalidated. If you encounter such reactions, it's okay to limit your interactions with these individuals or to adjust the level of detail you share with them. Focus your energy on those who genuinely understand and support your healing journey.

In addition to personal support networks, exploring professional resources can be instrumental in creating a more robust support system. A therapist specializing in trauma and stress management can provide a safe and confidential space to process your experiences, develop coping strategies, and address underlying issues contributing to your stress. Therapists can equip you with tools and techniques to navigate challenging emotions and develop resilience in the face of adversity. They can also help you identify and address unhealthy patterns in your relationships and interactions.

Different therapeutic approaches can be beneficial depending on individual needs. Cognitive Behavioral Therapy (CBT) focuses on identifying and modifying negative thought patterns, while Eye Movement Desensitization and Reprocessing (EMDR) is particularly effective in treating trauma-related symptoms. Somatic Experiencing (SE) focuses on addressing the body's physical responses to trauma, and mindfulness-based therapies emphasize the cultivation of present-moment awareness to reduce stress and enhance self-regulation.

Finding the right therapist requires careful consideration. Many therapists specialize in specific areas, and it's important to find one whose approach aligns with your needs and preferences. Don't hesitate to schedule consultations with several therapists before making a decision. A good therapeutic relationship is built on trust and mutual respect, and it's essential to find a therapist with whom you feel comfortable and safe. Your comfort level with your therapist is critical to the success of therapy.

Beyond therapy, there are numerous additional resources available, such as support groups, educational workshops, and online communities focused on trauma and stress management. These resources can offer a sense of community, shared experiences, and access to practical strategies for coping with stress and trauma. The shared experiences of others in similar situations can be profoundly validating, reducing feelings of isolation and increasing hope.

A key component of creating a safe environment is proactively managing triggers and stressful situations. Triggers are specific stimuli that evoke painful memories and intense emotional responses. Identifying your triggers is the first step in developing effective coping strategies. Common triggers might include specific places, people, sounds, smells, or even particular thoughts or feelings. Once you've identified your triggers, you can develop strategies to minimize your exposure to them or to manage your reactions when they occur.

This might involve actively avoiding certain situations or locations, preparing coping statements in advance, employing mindfulness techniques to regulate your emotional responses, or seeking support from a trusted individual. For example, if a particular song is a trigger, you might remove it from your playlist. If social gatherings are overwhelming, you might limit your attendance or leave early if you start feeling overwhelmed. Experiment with different techniques to determine what works best for you and remember to be patient with yourself throughout the process. Healing is not a race; it's a journey.

The act of creating a safe and supportive environment is an ongoing process, requiring continuous attention and adaptation. It's not a one-time fix but a dynamic interplay between internal and external factors. Regular self-reflection, honest communication with loved ones, and a commitment to seeking professional help when needed are all essential components of this ongoing process. Remember that building a secure environment takes time and patience. Celebrate your progress, acknowledge your challenges, and approach the process with the same self-compassion you're cultivating within. By consistently nurturing this external support system, you provide a firm foundation for your healing journey, allowing you to build resilience and navigate the challenges of trauma and stress with greater ease and confidence. The ultimate goal is not merely to survive but to thrive, to rediscover joy, and to build a life filled with meaning and purpose.

Chapter 2: Cultivating Mindfulness

Building that secure external environment, as previously discussed, is a crucial step in your healing journey. However, even the most supportive external structure can't fully protect you from the internal storms of trauma and stress. This is where the power of mindfulness comes into play. Mindfulness acts as an internal anchor, a stabilizing force that helps you navigate these emotional currents with greater calm and clarity. It's not about ignoring your pain or suppressing your emotions; rather, it's about cultivating a relationship with your inner experience that's characterized by acceptance, curiosity, and compassion.

Mindfulness, at its core, is the practice of paying attention to the present moment without judgment. It's about noticing your thoughts, feelings, and bodily sensations as they arise, without getting swept away by them. It's a simple yet profound concept, one that can have a transformative impact on your ability to manage stress, regulate your emotions, and heal from trauma. The key is consistent practice. Like any skill, mindfulness takes time and dedication to develop. But even brief moments of mindful awareness can bring significant benefits.

One of the most fundamental mindfulness practices is breath awareness. It's a technique that can be practiced anytime, anywhere, requiring nothing more than your own breath. To begin, find a comfortable position, whether sitting, lying down, or even standing. Close your eyes gently, if that feels comfortable. Turn your attention to the sensation of your breath entering and leaving your body. Notice the rise and fall of your chest or abdomen. Don't try to change your breathing; simply observe it.

As you focus on your breath, you'll likely notice other sensations, thoughts, or emotions arising. This is perfectly normal. When this happens, simply acknowledge them without judgment, and gently redirect your attention back to your breath. Imagine your breath as an anchor, tethering you to the present moment. Each inhale and exhale brings you back to the here and now, grounding you in the present. Even a few minutes of breath awareness can calm your nervous system, reduce feelings of anxiety, and bring a sense of peace and stability.

Another powerful mindfulness practice is the body scan meditation. This involves systematically bringing your attention to different parts of your body, noticing any sensations without judgment. Begin by lying down comfortably. Close your eyes and bring your attention to your toes. Notice any sensations—tingling, warmth, pressure, or coolness. Don't try to change these sensations; simply observe them.

Slowly move your awareness up your body, paying attention to each part—your feet, ankles, calves, knees, thighs, hips, abdomen, chest, back, shoulders, arms, hands, fingers, neck, face, and head. As you scan your body, you might notice areas of tension or discomfort. Again, don't try to force any changes; simply acknowledge these sensations with curiosity and compassion. The body scan is a way of deepening your connection with your physical self, increasing your body awareness, and learning to recognize the subtle signals your body sends you.

Mindful movement offers another avenue for cultivating mindfulness. This might involve activities like yoga, tai chi, or even a simple walking meditation. The key is to pay attention to the sensations of your body as you move, noticing the feeling of your feet on the ground, the movement of your limbs, and the flow of your breath. Mindful movement helps to integrate the mind and body, creating a sense of grounding and presence.

Walking meditation, for example, is a remarkably effective practice. Find a quiet space where you can walk slowly and deliberately. Focus your attention on the sensations of your feet making contact with the ground. Notice the rhythm of your steps, the movement of your body, and the flow of your breath. As thoughts or distractions arise, acknowledge them without judgment and gently redirect your attention back to the sensations of walking. The simple act of walking can become a profound mindfulness practice, bringing you into deeper connection with the present moment.

The concept of "anchor points" is central to mindfulness. These are specific sensory experiences that help to ground you in the present moment. Your breath is a primary anchor point, but you can also use other senses. This could be the feeling of your feet on the ground, the sound of birds singing, the taste of your food, or the smell of fresh air. By consciously focusing on these anchor points, you can create a sense of stability and presence, even amidst chaos and distress.

Developing a mindfulness practice is a journey, not a destination. Start small. Begin with just a few minutes of breath awareness each day, gradually increasing the duration as you become more comfortable. Explore different mindfulness practices, finding those that resonate most with you. Consistency is key. Regular practice, even for short periods, will cultivate your ability to stay present and to manage stress and emotions more effectively.

It's also crucial to cultivate a non-judgmental attitude toward your experiences. Mindfulness is not about achieving a state of perfect serenity; it's about accepting your thoughts, feelings, and sensations as they are, without trying to change or suppress them. Judgement only adds another layer of suffering on top of whatever you're already feeling. Cultivating self-compassion is vital during this practice.

Moreover, consider keeping a mindfulness journal. After your practice, write down your experience. What did you notice about your breath, your body, your thoughts, or your emotions? What challenges did you encounter? What did you learn? This journal can serve as a record of your progress and a space for reflection and self-discovery.

Another important aspect is to integrate mindfulness into your daily life. Try to bring mindful awareness to everyday activities, such as eating, showering, or listening to music. Notice the details – the taste of your food, the warmth of the water, or the melody of the music. By cultivating mindfulness in this way, you'll begin to see the world with fresh eyes, appreciating the simple beauty of everyday moments.

Remember that the practice of mindfulness is not about escaping your problems or ignoring your pain. Rather, it's about learning to relate to your experience with greater clarity, compassion, and acceptance. It's about developing the ability to observe your thoughts and emotions without being controlled by them. This enables you to respond to challenges with greater skill and resilience.

Mindfulness isn't a quick fix, it's a long-term investment in your well-being. There will be times when your mind wanders, when you get caught up in thoughts and feelings. That's perfectly okay. Gently redirect your attention back to your anchor point and continue the practice. With consistent effort, you will gradually develop the capacity to be more present, more aware, and more in control of your emotional responses. This inner strength will greatly enhance your ability to navigate the challenges of trauma and stress with greater grace and resilience. It is a skill that will benefit you throughout your life.

Over time, you'll discover that mindfulness is not just a technique for managing stress; it's a way of living. It's a way of relating to yourself and the world with greater presence, compassion, and understanding. It's a journey of self-discovery, one that can lead to profound personal growth and a deeper sense of peace and well-being. Remember to be patient and kind to yourself throughout this process; self-compassion is essential. Celebrate your progress, no matter how small, and remember that each moment of mindful awareness is a step towards healing and wholeness. The journey toward healing is a marathon, not a sprint. Embrace the process, celebrate your successes, and learn from your challenges. You are worthy of peace and healing.

Mindful movement bridges the gap between the internal world of thoughts and emotions and the external world of our physical bodies. It's a powerful tool for trauma recovery because it allows us to directly engage with the physical manifestations of stress and trauma, often held within the body as tension, tightness, or pain. Unlike purely meditative practices that focus primarily on mental awareness, mindful movement integrates both mental and physical awareness, fostering a deeper sense of embodiment and self-regulation.

Yoga, with its emphasis on breathwork and mindful movement through various poses (asanas), provides an excellent example of this integration. Each pose invites us to pay attention to the subtle sensations in our muscles, joints, and connective tissues. Are we holding tension in our shoulders? Is there a tightness in our hips? The practice isn't about achieving the "perfect" pose, but rather about cultivating an awareness of the body's present state, without judgment. If a pose feels too intense, we modify it; if it feels too easy, we deepen it. The breath serves as a vital anchor, guiding us through the movement and helping us to regulate our nervous system. For example, in a forward bend (Uttanasana), we might focus on the lengthening sensation in our hamstrings as we exhale, and the release of tension in our shoulders as we inhale.

Tai chi, another deeply therapeutic mindful movement practice, emphasizes slow, deliberate movements, often accompanied by deep, rhythmic breathing. Its gentle, flowing sequences promote relaxation, improve balance and coordination, and cultivate a sense of inner calm. The focus on smooth, continuous transitions between postures fosters a sense of fluidity and helps to release stagnant energy. The mindful awareness of body sensations guides each movement, preventing any forceful or jarring actions. For example, the "brush knee" movement requires slow, deliberate attention to the weight shift, the rotation of the hips, and the subtle engagement of the abdominal muscles. This controlled movement fosters both physical and mental clarity.

Qigong, originating from traditional Chinese medicine, combines gentle movements, meditation, and breathwork to cultivate and harmonize the flow of qi (vital energy) through the body. Its emphasis on slow, intentional movements and focused breathing helps to regulate the nervous system, reduce stress, and enhance overall well-being. Each movement is imbued with intention, directing the energy flow and promoting relaxation. Practitioners may visualize the energy moving through meridians, focusing on sensations of warmth, coolness, or tingling as they perform movements. For instance, the "spinal cord breathing" exercise in Qigong, where one focuses on the breath traveling along the spine, fosters a deep connection with the body and promotes a sense of groundedness.

Regardless of the chosen mindful movement practice, certain principles remain constant. The first is the cultivation of non-judgmental awareness. We simply observe the sensations in our bodies without labeling them as "good" or "bad," "pleasant" or "unpleasant." The body is a landscape of sensations, and our role is to be an attentive observer, not a judge. Second, we embrace the principle of gradual progression. We begin with movements that are appropriate to our current physical capabilities and gradually increase the intensity and duration of the practice as our strength, flexibility, and awareness grow. For those with limited mobility, chair yoga or seated qigong can be highly beneficial, offering a way to cultivate mindfulness and body awareness without the need for extensive physical exertion. The goal is not to push our bodies to their limits, but rather to deepen our connection with them.

Specific modifications can be made to tailor any of these practices to individual needs and limitations. For example, individuals with back pain might modify yoga poses by using props like blocks or blankets to support their bodies, thereby reducing strain and promoting comfort. Those with limited range of motion can focus on simpler movements, and those with arthritis might need to adjust the pace and intensity of their practice. The key is to find a level of intensity that feels both challenging and sustainable. The practice should be enjoyable, promoting a sense of well-being and reducing stress.

Beyond the formal practices of yoga, tai chi, and qigong, we can incorporate mindful movement into everyday activities. Consider paying attention to the sensations in your feet as you walk, the movement of your arms as you wash dishes, or the stretch in your muscles as you reach for something on a high shelf. By bringing mindful awareness to these everyday movements, we cultivate a deeper sense of presence and connection with our bodies. Even small adjustments to our posture throughout the day, like regularly engaging the core muscles to maintain good posture, can make a significant difference in reducing physical tension and improving mental well-being.

This mindful approach to movement extends beyond physical postures. It also encompasses the quality of our movement. Are we rushing through our actions or are we moving with intention and awareness? Often, we move through our days on autopilot, oblivious to the subtle cues from our bodies. Mindful movement helps to bring us back into conscious awareness of our physical sensations, allowing us to respond to these cues appropriately. This, in turn, cultivates a deeper sense of body wisdom and a greater capacity for self-regulation. Our body becomes a source of information, not just a vessel for action.

The integration of mindfulness into our movement practices, whatever form they may take, yields profound benefits for those dealing with trauma and stress. The increased body awareness helps to identify and release physical tension that may be holding onto emotional pain. The focus on present-moment sensations anchors us in the here and now, reducing the likelihood of being overwhelmed by past traumas or future anxieties. The rhythmic breathing that often accompanies mindful movement further helps to regulate the nervous system, promoting a sense of calm and stability. The gentle movements can be particularly helpful for individuals who find intense exercise triggering or overwhelming.

Furthermore, mindful movement practices foster a sense of self-compassion. When we approach movement with kindness and acceptance, we create a space for self-healing. We acknowledge our limitations without judgment, recognizing that our bodies are capable of incredible things, yet also require care and respect. The feeling of self-acceptance nurtured through mindful movement extends beyond the practice itself, permeating into other areas of our lives.

In essence, mindful movement isn't just about physical exercise; it's a profound practice in self-connection, self-regulation, and self-compassion. It's a pathway toward healing and wholeness, enabling us to cultivate a healthier relationship with our bodies and minds, particularly for those navigating the complexities of trauma and stress. It's an ongoing journey of discovery, a process of learning to listen to the wisdom of our bodies and responding with care and understanding. By consistently attending to the subtle cues of our bodies, we cultivate resilience, enhance emotional regulation, and foster a deeper connection to our authentic selves. The journey itself is the reward.

Mindful self-compassion is a powerful antidote to the harsh self-criticism and judgment that often accompany trauma and stress. It involves turning our attention inward with kindness, offering ourselves the same understanding and care we would offer a dear friend facing similar challenges. This isn't about ignoring our difficulties or pretending everything is fine; rather, it's about acknowledging our suffering with empathy and compassion, without judgment or self-blame.

The cornerstone of mindful self-compassion is the cultivation of self-awareness. We begin by noticing our thoughts and feelings without getting swept away by them. If we find ourselves caught in a cycle of negative self-talk, we gently redirect our attention to the present moment, acknowledging our experience without judgment. This might involve focusing on our breath, noticing the sensations in our body, or simply observing the thoughts as they arise and pass without engaging with them.

One effective technique is the "Mindful Body Scan." This involves systematically bringing our attention to different parts of the body, noticing any sensations without judgment. We start by noticing the sensations in our feet, paying attention to any tingling, warmth, pressure, or tension. We then move our awareness slowly up the body, noticing sensations in our ankles, calves, knees, thighs, and so on. Throughout this process, we maintain a posture of kindness and acceptance towards our body, acknowledging any discomfort without resistance or criticism.

Another useful exercise is the "Loving-Kindness Meditation." This meditation involves repeating phrases of loving-kindness, starting with ourselves and then extending them to others. We might begin by silently repeating phrases like "May I be filled with loving-kindness," "May I be healthy and strong," "May I be peaceful and serene." After spending a few minutes directing these phrases toward ourselves, we can extend them to loved ones, then to acquaintances, then to neutral people, and finally, to difficult people. This practice helps to cultivate a sense of connection and compassion not only toward ourselves but also towards others.

Furthermore, the "Three-Minute Breathing Space" is a simple yet potent technique to incorporate into daily life. It requires just three minutes and can be practiced anywhere, anytime. Begin by sitting comfortably, closing your eyes if that feels comfortable, and turning your attention to your breath. Observe the natural rhythm of your inhales and exhales, without trying to change it. Then, broaden your awareness to include the sensations in your body, noticing any tension or discomfort without judgment. Finally, expand your awareness further to include your thoughts and emotions, acknowledging them without getting carried away. This practice helps ground you in the present moment and cultivate a sense of self-awareness that is essential for mindful self-compassion.

For those grappling with intense emotions, the "Self-Compassion Break" can be particularly helpful. This technique involves acknowledging difficult emotions and offering ourselves self-compassion. When we experience intense emotions, we start by acknowledging them without judgment. For example, we might say to ourselves, "I'm feeling overwhelmed right now," or "I'm feeling really sad." Then, we remind ourselves that everyone experiences difficult emotions at times. Finally, we offer ourselves kindness and support, perhaps by saying, "It's okay to feel this way," or "I'm here for myself." This simple exercise allows us to approach difficult emotions with empathy rather than self-criticism.

Beyond these formal exercises, we can weave mindful self-compassion into our daily lives through simple acts of self-care. This might involve taking a warm bath, listening to soothing music, spending time in nature, or engaging in a hobby we enjoy. The key is to choose activities that nourish our bodies, minds, and spirits. These acts of self-care aren't selfish indulgences; they are essential for maintaining our well-being and cultivating a sense of self-compassion.

A crucial aspect of mindful self-compassion is the practice of self-acceptance. This involves acknowledging our imperfections and vulnerabilities without judgment. We all make mistakes; we all have flaws. Self-acceptance is not about denying our imperfections but about acknowledging them with kindness and compassion. This may involve reframing negative self-talk, challenging harsh inner critics, and celebrating our strengths and accomplishments. A helpful exercise is to write down a list of your strengths, both big and small, and then reflect on these qualities. This can help shift your focus from your perceived shortcomings to your inherent worth.

The cultivation of self-worth is another essential component of mindful self-compassion. This involves recognizing our inherent value as human beings, regardless of our accomplishments or perceived failures. We are worthy of love, respect, and compassion simply because we exist. This recognition is not contingent upon external validation or achievement; it is an intrinsic aspect of our being. Journaling can be a powerful tool to explore this, prompting yourself with questions like: "What are my core values? How can I better align my actions with these values? What small act of kindness can I offer myself today?"

It's important to remember that mindful self-compassion is a practice, not a destination. It takes time and effort to cultivate this skill. There will be times when we slip into self-criticism or judgment. When this happens, we gently redirect our attention back to self-compassion, recognizing that these moments are part of the process. We can treat these lapses in self-compassion with the same understanding and kindness we would extend to a friend.

Furthermore, practicing mindful self-compassion isn't about ignoring our problems or avoiding difficult emotions. It's about acknowledging our struggles while offering ourselves kindness and support. By shifting from a critical to a compassionate stance toward ourselves, we create space for healing and growth. This allows us to process our experiences with greater clarity and develop healthy coping mechanisms.

The integration of mindful self-compassion with mindful movement creates a synergistic effect, enhancing the therapeutic benefits of both practices. The body awareness cultivated through movement helps us to notice physical sensations associated with difficult emotions, while the self-compassion helps us to approach these sensations with kindness and acceptance, rather than resistance or avoidance. For example, after a mindful movement session, notice any lingering tension in your body and gently offer it acceptance and care.

Mindful self-compassion is not a quick fix; it's a journey of self-discovery and self-acceptance. It's a continuous process of learning to treat ourselves with the same kindness, patience, and understanding that we would offer a close friend facing similar difficulties. By consistently practicing mindful self-compassion, we cultivate resilience, enhance our emotional regulation, and foster a deeper connection to our authentic selves. The journey itself is a testament to our strength and courage, a process of healing and self-discovery that leads to a more fulfilling and compassionate life. The regular practice of these exercises, combined with consistent self-reflection, can transform our relationship with ourselves, fostering inner peace and a greater sense of well-being. The path towards self-compassion is paved with small, consistent steps, each one bringing us closer to a more compassionate and fulfilling life.

Our minds are naturally restless. They flit from one thought to another, a continuous stream of consciousness that rarely settles on a single point. This is especially true when we attempt to quiet the mind, as in meditation. The frustration that arises when our minds wander during mindfulness practice is a common experience, not a sign of failure. In fact, the very act of noticing the mind wandering and gently guiding it back to the present moment is a crucial aspect of the mindfulness training itself. This is where the power of self-compassion truly shines.

Imagine trying to hold a handful of quicksilver. The more tightly you clench your fist, the more it slips through your fingers. Similarly, the harder we try to force our minds to stay still, the more likely they are to resist. The key is to approach this challenge with gentleness and acceptance, recognizing that mind-wandering is an inherent part of the human experience. Instead of fighting our thoughts, we learn to observe them with curiosity and compassion, acknowledging them without judgment.

One effective strategy is to utilize a mantra. A mantra is a word, phrase, or sound repeated silently or aloud to anchor your attention. It could be a simple word like "peace," "calm," or "breathe," or a short phrase that resonates with you, such as "I am present," or "Let go and be." The mantra acts as a lighthouse in a storm, a beacon guiding your attention back to the present moment when your mind strays. The repetition itself isn't the goal; it's a gentle means of redirecting your focus, like gently nudging a child back to a task. When you notice your thoughts drifting, simply return to your chosen mantra without self-criticism.

Another helpful approach is to acknowledge the thought without judgment. When you notice your mind has wandered, instead of reprimanding yourself or trying to suppress the thought, simply acknowledge it. You might silently say to yourself, "Oh, there's a thought," or "My mind has wandered." This act of recognition is a crucial step in releasing the thought's grip on your attention. Try not to analyze the thought or engage with its content; simply acknowledge its presence and gently redirect your attention back to your breath or the sensations in your body. This process is akin to watching clouds drift across the sky; you acknowledge their presence, but you don't try to grasp them or change their course.

The breath itself becomes a powerful anchor. When distractions arise, gently turn your attention back to the sensation of your breath entering and leaving your body. Feel the cool air on your nostrils as you inhale and the warmth as you exhale. Notice the rise and fall of your abdomen or chest. The breath is always present, a constant and reliable point of reference amidst the ever-changing landscape of our thoughts and emotions. Even subtle sensations – a slight tingling in your fingertips, the weight of your body against the chair, or a faint pulse in your wrist – can serve as anchors to bring you back to the present moment.

Cultivating patience is also essential in overcoming mind-wandering. Mindfulness is a practice, not a performance. There is no such thing as a "perfect" meditation. The more you practice, the more skillful you become at recognizing and redirecting your attention. Expect your mind to wander. It's not a sign of failure; it's an opportunity to practice. Each time your mind wanders and you gently guide it back, you strengthen your capacity for focus and attention. Embrace the imperfections, celebrate the effort, and approach the practice with self-compassion. Treat yourself with the same kindness and understanding you would offer a friend struggling with a similar challenge.

It can be helpful to set realistic expectations. Begin with shorter meditation sessions, perhaps five or ten minutes, and gradually increase the duration as your ability to focus improves. Don't get discouraged if your mind wanders frequently. It's normal. The goal isn't to eliminate thoughts entirely; it's to cultivate a greater awareness of them and a gentler way of interacting with them. Remember, the process itself is a form of meditation. The journey is as valuable as the destination.

Somatic practices can provide a powerful complement to mindfulness meditation in managing mind-wandering. Since mind-wandering often stems from underlying tension or anxiety, addressing this physical aspect can significantly reduce its frequency. Gentle stretching, yoga, or even mindful walking can help release physical tension, thereby calming the nervous system and creating a more receptive state for meditation. By bringing awareness to your body, you connect with the present moment, grounding you in a tangible experience that is less susceptible to the pull of wandering thoughts. Paying close attention to the physical sensations in your body can help bring you back to the present whenever your mind drifts off.

Another helpful technique is to incorporate visualization into your meditation practice. Imagine a calm and peaceful scene, perhaps a tranquil beach, a lush forest, or a quiet mountaintop. Engage your senses in this scene, noticing the colors, sounds, smells, and textures. This creates a mental image that can act as an anchor, drawing your attention back to the present when your mind starts to wander. The more vivid and detailed your visualization, the more effective it will be. The key is to immerse yourself in the sensory experience, engaging not only your mind but also your imagination.

Consider keeping a journal to record your meditation experiences. This practice offers valuable insights into your progress and helps to identify patterns in your mind-wandering. Note the frequency of your distractions, the types of thoughts that most commonly arise, and the effectiveness of different strategies in redirecting your attention. This self-reflection allows you to adapt your practice to better suit your individual needs and preferences. It provides a space for self-compassionate observation, acknowledging your progress and areas for improvement without judgment. This process is not about self-criticism but about self-understanding.

Mindfulness is not about stopping thoughts; it's about changing our relationship with them. It's about learning to observe them without judgment, acknowledging their presence without getting swept away by their content. The key is to approach this process with patience, self-compassion, and a sense of humor. Treat your mind-wandering as an opportunity for practice, not a sign of failure. Each time you gently guide your attention back to the present moment, you are strengthening your capacity for focus, cultivating self-awareness, and developing a more compassionate relationship with yourself. The journey is a process of continuous learning and refinement. Be kind to yourself along the way. Mindfulness is not a destination, but a path, and every step is progress. The path is the practice, and the practice is where the true transformation lies. Embrace the journey.

Building on the foundation of formal mindfulness practice, we now turn our attention to integrating these principles into the fabric of daily life. The goal isn't to carve out extensive periods for meditation, but rather to cultivate a mindful awareness that permeates our interactions with the world, moment by moment. This means transforming ordinary activities – eating, walking, working – into opportunities for presence and grounding. The beauty of this approach lies in its accessibility; it doesn't require special equipment or secluded spaces. It simply requires a shift in perspective, a conscious decision to engage fully with the present experience.

Let's begin with the seemingly mundane act of eating. How often do we consume meals while simultaneously checking emails, scrolling through social media, or engaging in conversation that distracts us from the actual experience of eating? Mindful eating invites us to savor each bite, paying attention to the texture, taste, and smell of the food. Notice the temperature, the way the food feels in your mouth, the subtle nuances of flavor that might otherwise go unnoticed. Slow down your eating pace, chew thoroughly, and allow yourself to appreciate the nourishment the food provides, both physically and emotionally. Put away all distractions; this is a moment for you and your meal. This seemingly simple act can be a profound meditation, grounding you in the present moment and fostering a deeper connection with your body and the food you consume. Try focusing on just one food at a time, and if you find your mind wandering to thoughts of your to-do list, simply acknowledge the thought without judgment and gently redirect your attention back to the taste and texture of your food.

Extending this mindful approach to walking is similarly transformative. Instead of rushing through your day, transforming your commute or a leisurely stroll into a hurried blur, try to walk mindfully. Pay attention to the sensation of your feet on the ground, the rhythm of your steps, the movement of your body. Notice the subtle shifts in your posture, the way your breath flows with each stride. Engage your senses – observe the sights, sounds, and smells around you. Feel the sun on your skin, the wind in your hair, or the coolness of the shade. Walking mindfully becomes a moving meditation, a way to connect with your body and the environment around you. Notice details you may have missed before—the intricate patterns of leaves, the varied colors of the bark on trees, the way sunlight filters through the canopy. Walking mindfully is a pathway to increased presence in everyday life, reducing stress and anxiety while enhancing awareness and connection with oneself and the environment.

Integrating mindfulness into work requires a more nuanced approach. The demands of a busy workday often make it challenging to maintain a constant state of mindful awareness. However, even brief moments of mindfulness can significantly impact productivity and overall well-being. Take short breaks throughout your workday to practice mindfulness. These micro-breaks, as little as one to two minutes, can be powerfully rejuvenating. During these breaks, focus on your breath, the sensations in your body, or the sounds around you. You can also utilize visualization techniques, imagining a calming scene to help you detach from the pressures of work. If you're working on a computer, take a moment to consciously notice the feel of the keyboard under your fingertips, the rhythm of your typing. Even amidst the demands of your tasks, moments of mindful attention can create a sense of calm and grounding that enhances focus and creativity. If a task is particularly stressful, try focusing on your breathing or using a mantra such as "calm and focused" to recenter your energy.

Furthermore, extending mindful principles to our interactions with others can profoundly enrich our relationships. Instead of reacting automatically to situations or engaging in passive listening, we can cultivate conscious and intentional engagement. Truly listen to the other person, focusing on their words and emotions without interrupting or formulating your response. Be present in the conversation, noticing not just the content of the words but also the nuances in tone and body language. This mindful approach fosters genuine connection and understanding. Notice the expressions on their face, the tone of their voice, the subtle cues that communicate feelings beyond words. Respond thoughtfully and intentionally, offering empathy and compassion. Conscious communication allows for deeper understanding and connection, leading to more meaningful relationships and minimizing conflict.

It's crucial to acknowledge that integrating mindfulness into daily life is a journey, not a destination. There will be days when you feel more connected and present, and days when your mind wanders more frequently. This is perfectly normal. The key is to approach the practice with patience, self-compassion, and a willingness to experiment with different techniques to find what resonates with you. Don't strive for perfection; strive for progress. Celebrate small victories and acknowledge the challenges without self-criticism. The very act of making the effort is a testament to your commitment to self-care and growth. Remember that setbacks are opportunities for learning and refinement, not reasons to give up. Each time you gently redirect your attention back to the present moment, you're strengthening your capacity for mindfulness.

One valuable strategy is to establish daily routines that incorporate mindfulness practices. This could involve setting aside a few minutes each morning for meditation or mindful breathing before starting your day. Or perhaps you could incorporate mindful moments into your evening routine, using a calming activity like taking a warm bath or engaging in gentle stretches. These consistent practices reinforce the habit of mindfulness and create a sense of grounding and calm. It's about building mindful moments into the tapestry of your daily life, not necessarily dedicating large blocks of time.

Experiment with different approaches. Some individuals find that listening to calming music while performing routine tasks enhances their mindfulness. Others may find that working with their hands – knitting, gardening, or cooking – promotes a sense of presence. The possibilities are endless. The key is to identify activities that help you cultivate a sense of calm and focus, and then consciously incorporate them into your day. You might even try mindful cleaning, focusing on the sensations of the cleaning products in your hands, the movement of the cleaning tools, or the transformation of a messy space into a tidy one. The key is to find techniques and activities that you enjoy and that support your specific needs and preferences.

Finally, remember that self-compassion is paramount. Integrating mindfulness into daily life is not a performance, and there is no such thing as "perfect" mindfulness. There will be days when your attention drifts, when distractions overwhelm you, and when you struggle to maintain presence. Be kind to yourself during these times; treat yourself with the same understanding and empathy you would offer a friend facing similar challenges. Acknowledge your effort and progress, and gently redirect your attention back to the present moment without self-recrimination. The journey of cultivating mindfulness is a lifelong process, a continuous evolution of awareness and self-understanding. Embrace the imperfections and celebrate every step of the way. Your commitment to this practice is a testament to your strength and self-compassion. The journey itself is the practice, and within that journey lies a profound capacity for growth and transformation.

Chapter 3: Reframing Your Narrative

Building upon the mindful practices explored in the previous section, we now delve into the crucial task of identifying and reframing limiting beliefs. These beliefs, often deeply ingrained and unconscious, act as significant obstacles on the path to healing and recovery from trauma. They represent ingrained negative narratives about ourselves, others, and the world, shaping our perceptions, reactions, and ultimately, our lives. Recognizing and challenging these beliefs is a pivotal step towards reclaiming agency and fostering emotional well-being.

Many of these limiting beliefs originate in early childhood experiences. The messages we receive from caregivers, peers, and societal influences can profoundly impact our self-perception and our ability to navigate challenges. A child frequently told they are "stupid" or "bad" may internalize these labels, developing a deep-seated belief in their own inadequacy. Similarly, a child who experiences neglect or abuse may develop a belief that they are unworthy of love or connection, leading to difficulties forming healthy relationships later in life. These early experiences, whether overtly negative or subtly undermining, create a foundation of belief that can significantly impact how we interpret events and interact with the world throughout our lives.

Identifying these deeply ingrained beliefs often requires introspection and self-compassion. It's not a process of self-criticism, but rather a gentle exploration of the patterns that have shaped our experiences. Journaling can be an invaluable tool. Take some time to reflect on recurring negative thoughts or feelings. What are the underlying beliefs driving these emotions? For example, the feeling of anxiety before a social event might stem from a belief that you are inherently awkward or unlikeable. The feeling of constant self-doubt could be rooted in the belief that you are not capable or intelligent enough. The critical self-talk you experience might be reflective of a belief that you are fundamentally flawed. Identifying these beliefs is the first step to challenging their validity and constructing a more supportive internal narrative.

Consider exploring past experiences that may have contributed to these beliefs. Reflect on specific events or interactions that reinforced these negative patterns. Was there a specific instance where you felt deeply criticized or rejected? Was there a time when your capabilities were underestimated or dismissed? These recollections can offer valuable insights into the origins of your limiting beliefs, allowing you to begin to understand the context in which they were formed.

Remember that these beliefs are not immutable truths. They are interpretations, often distorted or exaggerated by the emotional lens of past experiences. The process of identifying them isn't about uncovering some inherent flaw; instead it's about understanding how past trauma shaped your internal landscape. Trauma often leads to cognitive distortions, which are inaccurate or unhelpful ways of thinking that contribute to mental and emotional distress. These distortions can manifest in various ways, including all-or-nothing thinking (viewing situations as entirely good or bad), overgeneralization (drawing sweeping conclusions based on limited evidence), mental filtering (focusing only on negative aspects and ignoring positive ones), and catastrophizing (expecting the worst possible outcome). Understanding these cognitive distortions is key to challenging and ultimately replacing them with more balanced and realistic perspectives.

Let's examine some common limiting beliefs associated with trauma:

"I am unworthy of love and connection." This belief often stems from experiences of neglect, abuse, or rejection. It can manifest as self-sabotaging behaviors in relationships, a fear of intimacy, and a deep-seated feeling of loneliness, even amidst supportive relationships. Challenging this belief requires actively cultivating self-compassion and engaging in self-care practices. This might involve identifying and celebrating personal strengths and accomplishments, spending time with loved ones who demonstrate acceptance and appreciation, and actively seeking out healthy relationships. Remember, past experiences do not define your worthiness of love.

"I am incapable of achieving my goals." This belief, often born from past failures or experiences of powerlessness, can manifest as procrastination, avoidance of challenges, and self-doubt. Addressing this belief requires breaking down goals into smaller, manageable steps and celebrating each accomplishment along the way. It also involves actively challenging negative self-talk and building self-efficacy through gradual exposure to challenging situations. Remember, setbacks are temporary and do not invalidate your potential for success. Learn from each step and continue forward.

"I am unsafe and vulnerable." This belief, frequently associated with trauma, manifests as hypervigilance, anxiety, and a persistent sense of fear. Addressing this belief may require therapy and practical strategies to enhance your sense of safety and security, which might include implementing safety plans, developing coping mechanisms for anxiety, and seeking supportive relationships. Remember that safety is not a binary state; it is a spectrum that can be actively cultivated and enhanced.

"I am to blame for what happened." This belief is particularly common in individuals who have experienced trauma. It's crucial to understand that trauma is never the victim's fault. Challenging this belief often requires therapy to process the event and understand its impact. It requires separating oneself from the event's emotional weight and to learn about the role of trauma in causing such reactions. It also requires actively cultivating self-compassion and recognizing that trauma survivors are not responsible for the actions of others.

"I am broken and irreparably damaged." This belief is deeply ingrained in many trauma survivors. It is essential to challenge this belief by focusing on resilience and the capacity for healing. It's crucial to remember that healing from trauma is a process, not a destination. Celebrating small steps forward, recognizing personal strengths, and engaging in self-care practices are vital in challenging this limiting belief.

Once you have identified your limiting beliefs, the next step involves challenging their validity. This isn't about simply dismissing them; it's about critically examining the evidence that supports or refutes them. Ask yourself: What evidence do I have to support this belief? What evidence contradicts this belief? Are there alternative explanations for the experiences that led me to develop this belief? Often, these beliefs are based on distorted perceptions and lack concrete evidence. Challenging these beliefs often requires the support of a therapist, who can help you work through these negative thought patterns and develop more adaptive coping mechanisms.

Remember, reframing your narrative is not about erasing the past but about integrating it into a more complete and nuanced understanding of yourself. By acknowledging and challenging your limiting beliefs, you are actively participating in your own healing and growth. This process requires patience, self-compassion, and a willingness to engage in ongoing self-reflection. It is a journey of self-discovery, empowerment, and transformation. The strength you discover in this process will be a testament to your resilience and capacity for healing. The journey itself is transformative. The willingness to confront deeply ingrained beliefs and to actively challenge them empowers you to rewrite your internal story, moving from victim to survivor, from fear to empowerment. The mindfulness practices we explored earlier provide essential tools to support this ongoing process of self-discovery and healing. They equip you with the tools to manage the discomfort that naturally accompanies this work. By embracing the present moment with compassion and awareness, you create space for healing and growth.

Building on the foundation of mindful awareness and the identification of limiting beliefs, we now turn to practical techniques for cognitive restructuring. This involves actively challenging and reframing those ingrained negative thought patterns that perpetuate feelings of distress and hinder healing. Cognitive restructuring is not about ignoring or suppressing difficult emotions; rather, it's about gaining a more balanced and realistic perspective on your experiences, enabling you to respond to life's challenges with greater resilience and self-compassion.

One fundamental technique is

cognitive reframing, which involves identifying and re-evaluating the meaning you assign to events. Often, our initial interpretations are colored by emotional distress and past trauma, leading to distorted or exaggerated perceptions. Cognitive reframing encourages you to step back from this emotional reactivity and examine your thoughts more objectively. Consider a situation where you experienced a setback at work—perhaps a missed deadline or a critical comment from your supervisor. Your initial reaction might be to conclude that you are incompetent or a failure. Cognitive reframing encourages you to explore alternative interpretations. Perhaps the missed deadline was due to unforeseen circumstances, or the critical comment was intended to be constructive feedback. By considering multiple perspectives, you can replace the catastrophic interpretation of "I am a failure" with a more balanced and realistic assessment, such as, "This was a setback, but I can learn from it and improve my time management."

This process involves several key steps. First, you need to identify the negative automatic thoughts (NATs) that arise in response to triggering events. These are the spontaneous, often unconscious, thoughts that pop into your mind without conscious reflection. Pay close attention to your inner dialogue. What are the recurring themes? Are there patterns of negativity or self-criticism? Keeping a journal can be extremely helpful in tracking these NATs and identifying recurring patterns. Once identified, analyze the evidence supporting and contradicting these thoughts. Often, the evidence supporting a negative thought is minimal, while evidence contradicting it is far more substantial but may be overlooked due to emotional reactivity.

For example, let's say a NAT is "I'm unlovable." Now, examine the evidence. Do you have any relationships where people show love and affection for you? Have you experienced instances of kindness and support? Have you had moments where you were clearly loved, perhaps in childhood? By listing these instances, you build a counter-narrative to challenge the negative thought. If your evidence against the NAT is weak, examine the validity of the underlying beliefs and consider where those beliefs originated from. If the evidence seems insufficient, seek professional guidance. A therapist can help you systematically examine these beliefs and generate alternative explanations.

Another crucial technique is

challenging negative thoughts. This isn't about arguing with your thoughts or trying to suppress them, but rather about questioning their accuracy and validity. Use a Socratic questioning approach. Ask yourself: What is the evidence that supports this thought? Is there any other way to interpret this situation? What would I tell a friend who had this thought? Often, we are far more compassionate and understanding towards others than we are towards ourselves. By shifting your perspective, you can identify flaws in your logic and develop a more compassionate self-response.

Let's say you have the thought "I'm a failure because I didn't get that promotion." You can challenge this by asking: What is the evidence that this one event defines my entire worth? Are there other accomplishments I've achieved? What are my strengths and skills? What can I learn from this experience to improve my chances in the future? By systematically questioning the accuracy and validity of your negative thoughts, you can gradually replace them with more realistic and balanced ones.

A powerful adjunct to cognitive reframing is

cognitive behavioral therapy (CBT), a widely researched and effective approach that integrates cognitive and behavioral techniques. CBT focuses on the interplay between thoughts, feelings, and behaviors. By identifying and challenging maladaptive thoughts, you can modify your emotional responses and behavior. For instance, if fear of public speaking triggers avoidance behavior, CBT would address the underlying thoughts contributing to the fear—such as "I'll make a fool of myself" or "Everyone will judge me"—and work on developing strategies to challenge these thoughts and modify the behavior.

In addition to these individual techniques, incorporating

mindfulness practices can significantly enhance the effectiveness of cognitive restructuring. Mindfulness cultivates present-moment awareness, allowing you to observe your thoughts without judgment. This non-judgmental observation creates space between you and your thoughts, preventing identification with them. Rather than being swept away by negative thoughts, you can witness them as fleeting mental events, reducing their power to dictate your emotional state.

Furthermore, integrating

somatic practices into your cognitive restructuring process can be invaluable. Trauma often manifests in the body as tension, pain, or other physical sensations. Somatic practices, such as body scan meditations or gentle movement, can help you connect with these bodily sensations and release trapped energy. This can facilitate emotional regulation and reduce the intensity of emotional responses, creating a more conducive environment for engaging in cognitive reframing.

Remember, cognitive restructuring is not a quick fix. It requires consistent effort and self-compassion. There will be setbacks, and that's okay. The key is to maintain a commitment to the process, to practice regularly, and to seek support when needed. A therapist can provide guidance and support throughout this process, helping you identify limiting beliefs, develop effective strategies for challenging negative thoughts, and integrate these techniques into your daily life.

The benefits of cognitive restructuring extend far beyond simply changing negative thoughts. By reframing your narrative and cultivating more realistic and balanced perspectives, you build emotional resilience, enhance self-esteem, and improve your overall well-being. You become better equipped to handle life's challenges, navigating setbacks with greater grace and self-compassion. You move from a place of reactivity and distress to a place of agency and empowerment, actively shaping your own experience and fostering a life filled with purpose and meaning. This active engagement in rewriting your internal story is a profound act of self-healing and transformation, empowering you to create a future defined by hope, resilience, and lasting well-being. The journey might be challenging at times, but the rewards are well worth the effort. You are reclaiming your narrative, rewriting your story, and ultimately, reclaiming your life. The process is transformative, taking you from a state of feeling overwhelmed and trapped by the past to a state of empowerment and possibility. By embracing these tools and techniques, you are investing in your long-term mental and emotional health.

Building upon the techniques of cognitive reframing and challenging negative thoughts, journaling emerges as a powerful tool for self-discovery and emotional processing. It offers a safe and private space to explore the complexities of your inner world, unearthing hidden patterns and fostering self-understanding. Journaling is not merely about recording events; it's about actively engaging with your experiences, reflecting on their meaning, and cultivating self-compassion. The act of writing itself can be therapeutic, allowing you to externalize your thoughts and emotions, creating a distance that fosters objectivity and reduces the intensity of emotional overwhelm.

One particularly effective approach is

gratitude journaling. Each day, take a few moments to reflect on the positive aspects of your life, no matter how small. This simple practice shifts your focus from what's lacking to what you have, fostering a sense of appreciation and contentment. It's not about ignoring challenges, but rather about acknowledging the good alongside the bad, creating a more balanced perspective. Start by listing three things you are grateful for each day. These could be anything from the warmth of the sun on your skin to the support of a loved one, a successful project completion, or simply a quiet moment of peace. Over time, you might notice a gradual shift in your overall emotional state, a lessening of negativity, and an increased capacity for joy.

Don't underestimate the power of simple observations. Note the details of your day—the sights, sounds, smells, tastes, and textures that you experience. This mindful attention to the present moment helps to ground you in the here and now, reducing rumination on the past or anxiety about the future. These sensory details can also unlock unexpected emotional insights, revealing connections between your environment and your internal state that might otherwise go unnoticed. For example, a detailed description of a walk in nature might reveal underlying feelings of peace and calm you didn't fully realize. Similarly, describing a stressful interaction might reveal subtle physical tension or emotional reactivity you were suppressing.

Emotional journaling delves deeper into the emotional landscape. When you experience a strong emotion—whether it's joy, sadness, anger, or fear—take time to explore it in detail. Describe the situation that triggered the emotion, the physical sensations associated with it (e.g., tightness in your chest, rapid heartbeat), and the thoughts that ran through your mind. Don't censor yourself; allow yourself to fully express your feelings, even if they are uncomfortable or difficult. This process of emotional articulation can be remarkably cathartic, facilitating emotional processing and reducing emotional intensity. It allows you to understand the root cause of your emotional responses, rather than simply reacting to them. Consider adding questions to your emotional journaling entries, prompting further reflection. For example: What are the underlying beliefs or assumptions contributing to this emotion?

What unmet needs might be contributing to this feeling? What would a more compassionate response look like?

Free writing is another valuable technique. Set a timer for 5-10 minutes and simply write whatever comes to mind, without editing or censoring yourself. This stream-of-consciousness approach can unlock unconscious thoughts and feelings, revealing patterns and insights that you might not access through more structured journaling. It's a form of mental decluttering, allowing you to release pent-up emotions and mental clutter. Don't worry about grammar, punctuation, or creating coherent sentences; the focus is on the process of writing itself. You may be surprised by the unexpected ideas and insights that emerge. Even seemingly random thoughts can unlock deeper understanding upon reflection.

The effectiveness of journaling is further enhanced by incorporating prompts designed to stimulate self-reflection. Prompts can focus on specific aspects of your life, guiding your exploration of particular themes or challenges. For instance, you could reflect on a significant relationship, exploring its dynamics, challenges, and personal growth. You might journal about your career aspirations, identifying limiting beliefs and developing strategies for achieving your goals. Or you could focus on a specific trauma or stressful experience, exploring its impact on your life and how you have processed it. Regular reflection on these experiences can foster a deeper understanding of your own resilience and capacity for healing.

Consider these examples:

Relationship Prompt: "Describe a significant relationship in your life. What are its strengths and weaknesses? How has this relationship impacted your sense of self? What are your hopes and fears for the future of this relationship?"

Career Prompt: "What are your long-term career aspirations? What steps can you take to achieve these goals? What are your biggest fears or obstacles? How can you overcome them?"

Trauma Prompt (use with caution, potentially with professional support): "Reflect on a traumatic experience. What are your immediate memories and feelings associated with this event? How has this event impacted you physically, emotionally, and mentally? What steps have you already taken to heal, and what support do you need moving forward?" Remember to approach sensitive topics with caution and seek professional guidance if needed.

It's crucial to approach journaling with self-compassion. There's no right or wrong way to journal; the process is personal and unique to you. Don't get discouraged if you find it challenging at first. Start with short sessions, gradually increasing the time as you feel more comfortable. Experiment with different types of prompts and techniques, finding what works best for you. The goal is not to achieve perfection but to create a space for self-exploration and emotional processing. The consistency of the practice is key. The more you engage in journaling, the more insightful your self-discoveries will become, and the stronger your capacity for self-compassion will grow.

Beyond individual journaling exercises, consider the broader benefits of maintaining a consistent journaling practice. Over time, you might notice patterns in your thoughts and emotions, identifying recurring themes or triggers. This increased self-awareness can be incredibly powerful, enabling you to proactively manage your emotional responses and cultivate healthier coping mechanisms. By tracking your progress, you can also celebrate your successes and learn from your setbacks, reinforcing your commitment to self-growth and healing.

Furthermore, journaling provides a valuable record of your journey. Looking back on your entries over time can reveal significant personal growth, reminding you of your resilience and strength. This perspective shift can be especially beneficial during times of stress or challenge, providing a sense of hope and encouragement. It serves as a tangible representation of your progress, offering a source of reassurance and validation.

In conclusion, journaling is not a standalone therapy, but a valuable complement to other cognitive restructuring techniques. By combining journaling with mindful awareness, cognitive reframing, and somatic practices, you create a holistic approach to emotional healing and self-discovery. It is an active process of engaging with your inner world, fostering a deeper understanding of yourself and paving the way for lasting personal growth and resilience. Remember to be patient with yourself throughout this process; self-discovery is a journey, not a destination. Embrace the challenges, celebrate the small victories, and continue to explore the depths of your being through the powerful practice of journaling.

Building on the foundation of self-reflection established through journaling, we now turn to the powerful realm of creative expression as a pathway to healing from trauma and stress. While journaling offers a primarily verbal approach to processing emotions, creative expression taps into a broader spectrum of human experience, utilizing non-verbal channels to access and articulate what may be difficult to put into words. Trauma often manifests not only in thoughts and feelings but also in the body, leaving deep imprints on our physical and emotional selves. Creative outlets offer a unique opportunity to bypass the limitations of language and directly engage with these embodied experiences.

Art therapy, for instance, provides a rich landscape for exploring the complexities of trauma. Through painting, drawing, sculpting, or collage, individuals can externalize their internal experiences, giving form to emotions that might otherwise remain trapped within. The process itself is therapeutic; the act of creating, of applying color to canvas, of shaping clay into form, can be incredibly cathartic, offering a sense of control and agency in the face of overwhelming feelings. The resulting artwork isn't necessarily about creating a masterpiece; it's about the process of self-expression, of allowing the unconscious to manifest itself in tangible form.

Consider the potential of color, for instance. A vibrant red might represent intense anger or passion, while muted blues could symbolize sadness or withdrawal. The textures, shapes, and composition of the artwork can all hold symbolic meaning, reflecting the nuances of the individual's inner world. Working with a trained art therapist can provide guidance in interpreting these symbolic representations, facilitating deeper self-understanding and emotional processing. However, the process of creating art for self-healing can be equally effective without formal therapeutic guidance. The key is to approach it with curiosity and self-compassion, allowing the creative process to unfold organically.

Music therapy offers another powerful avenue for emotional expression and healing. Music has a unique capacity to evoke powerful emotions, tapping into deep-seated memories and experiences. Whether through playing an instrument, singing, or simply listening to music, individuals can use music as a tool for self-soothing, emotional regulation, and self-discovery. The rhythmic nature of music can be particularly grounding, helping to regulate the nervous system and reduce feelings of anxiety or overwhelm. Playing a musical instrument can be particularly empowering, offering a sense of control and mastery that can be especially valuable for those struggling with feelings of helplessness or vulnerability. Even listening to music that evokes specific emotions can be therapeutic, providing a safe and controlled way to experience and process these feelings.

For those who find visual arts or music less accessible, writing can be a potent tool for creative expression and emotional release. We've already explored journaling as a form of self-reflection, but creative writing extends this practice further, exploring narrative, imagery, and metaphor to convey complex emotions and experiences. This could involve writing poetry, short stories, or even dramatic monologues, allowing for a greater degree of artistic freedom and exploration. The focus shifts from the objective recording of facts to the subjective creation of a world, where emotions and experiences can be explored in a safe and controlled environment. The act of crafting a narrative allows the writer to step outside of their immediate experience, gaining a new perspective on their challenges and fostering greater self-understanding. Creative writing can be used to process traumatic events by transforming painful memories into a story, giving them a shape and narrative that reduces their power to overwhelm.

Beyond these established therapeutic modalities, consider other forms of creative expression. Dance, movement therapy, and drama are all valuable options, each providing unique opportunities for emotional release and self-discovery. Dance, in particular, can be a powerful tool for embodied expression, allowing individuals to release pent-up emotions through physical movement. Movement therapy similarly employs physical movement to access and process trauma, often focusing on releasing physical tension and restoring a sense of bodily awareness. Drama therapy, on the other hand, uses role-playing and improvisation to explore complex emotional issues, facilitating self-understanding and fostering resilience.

The choice of creative outlet is entirely personal; the most effective approach is the one that resonates most deeply with the individual. Experimentation is key; try different forms of creative expression until you discover what feels most natural and fulfilling. This might involve trying a single art class, joining a choir, enrolling in a creative writing workshop, taking a dance class, or even simply setting aside dedicated time each week for self-expression. The important thing is to begin. Don't aim for perfection; the focus is on the process, not the product. The act of creating itself is a form of self-care and self-healing.

To further enhance the therapeutic value of creative expression, consider integrating mindfulness practices. Mindful art-making, for instance, involves fully immersing yourself in the creative process, paying close attention to the sensations, emotions, and thoughts that arise. This mindful engagement amplifies the therapeutic effect of the creative activity, fostering deeper self-awareness and emotional regulation. Similarly, mindful movement practices can be incorporated into dance or movement therapy, promoting a greater sense of presence and grounding. By combining creative expression with mindfulness, you create a holistic approach to trauma recovery, utilizing both the emotional and physical dimensions of experience.

Furthermore, remember that creative expression is not a solitary endeavor. Sharing your work with others, whether through a supportive group, a therapist, or even close friends and family, can further enhance its therapeutic value. The act of sharing your creative work can be a deeply vulnerable experience, but it can also be incredibly empowering. It provides an opportunity to connect with others on a deeper level, fostering a sense of community and belonging. The feedback you receive, even criticism, can help you gain new perspectives on your work and your experiences. However, it is crucial to choose your audience carefully and to set appropriate boundaries to protect your emotional wellbeing.

It's crucial to acknowledge that the process of engaging with creative expression for healing can be challenging. It might unearth painful memories or emotions that have been suppressed for years. This is a normal part of the healing process, and it's important to approach it with self-compassion and patience. If you find the process overwhelming, don't hesitate to seek support from a mental health professional. A therapist can help you navigate the emotional challenges that may arise, provide a safe space for processing difficult experiences, and guide you in utilizing creative expression in a way that maximizes its therapeutic benefit.

In conclusion, creative expression serves as a powerful adjunct to cognitive reframing and other trauma-informed techniques. By allowing for nonverbal expression and tapping into the body's wisdom, it complements the analytical work of cognitive processing. It offers a diverse range of avenues for exploration, catering to individual preferences and needs. Remember that this process is deeply personal and requires patience and self-compassion. Embrace the journey of self-discovery, allowing your creativity to guide you towards healing and wholeness. The creation itself, irrespective of the final product, holds the transformative power; it's the journey, not the destination, that truly matters in this process of healing and self-discovery. The more you engage with these creative avenues, the more resilient you will become, strengthening your capacity for self-expression and self-acceptance.

Building upon the exploration of creative expression as a pathway to healing, we now delve into the crucial aspects of forgiveness and self-acceptance. These are not merely abstract concepts but vital components in the journey toward emotional well-being, particularly after experiencing trauma or prolonged stress. The capacity for self-compassion, a cornerstone of this process, intertwines deeply with the ability to forgive both oneself and others. Without self-compassion, the path to forgiveness can become fraught with self-judgment and impede the healing process.

Self-forgiveness is often the most challenging aspect. It demands acknowledging the mistakes we've made, accepting responsibility where appropriate, and ultimately releasing the burden of self-recrimination. This isn't about condoning harmful actions; rather, it's about recognizing our humanity, understanding that we are all fallible, and choosing to move forward rather than remaining trapped in a cycle of self-blame. The harsh inner critic, so often amplified by trauma, needs to be gently addressed, replaced with a voice of understanding and self-acceptance.

This process requires time and patience. It's not a linear journey; there will be setbacks, moments when old wounds resurface. Self-compassion acts as a buffer during these challenging times. Imagine speaking to a friend who has made a mistake. You wouldn't berate them; you'd likely offer empathy and support. Extend that same kindness to yourself. Practice self-soothing techniques when self-criticism arises, such as deep breathing exercises, mindful meditation, or engaging in a calming activity. Journaling can also be profoundly helpful, allowing you to express your feelings without judgment.

Consider reframing your narrative surrounding past mistakes. Instead of focusing solely on the negative aspects, explore the lessons learned, the growth experienced, and the resilience you demonstrated in overcoming the challenges. What strengths did you discover within yourself? What did you learn about your boundaries and needs? By focusing on the positive aspects of your experience, you gradually shift your perspective and create a more balanced and compassionate self-image.

Forgiveness of others is equally important, though often more readily discussed. Holding onto resentment and anger consumes immense emotional energy, perpetuating a cycle of negativity that hinders healing. Forgiving others does not mean condoning their actions, forgetting what happened, or even reconciling with them. It's about releasing the grip of anger and bitterness, freeing yourself from the emotional burden their actions have imposed on you.

This process is often facilitated by understanding the context of the other person's actions. It's not about excusing harmful behavior, but about recognizing the complexities of human experience, the influence of their own backgrounds, and the potential for their own pain and suffering to contribute to their actions. Empathy, even if it's difficult, can be a powerful tool in this process. Consider writing a letter to the person you need to forgive, expressing your feelings without sending it. This act of writing itself can be cathartic, allowing you to process your emotions and gain clarity.

Let go of the need for an apology. Many times, apologies are never forthcoming. Forgiveness, in these instances, becomes an act of self-liberation, a choice to release the emotional weight you carry. It is an act of prioritizing your own well-being and choosing to move forward. Holding onto the expectation of an apology keeps you tethered to the past, preventing you from fully embracing the present.

Letting go of resentment is a gradual process, requiring conscious effort and mindful practice. It's akin to releasing a heavy stone you've been carrying on your shoulders. The initial lightness might be subtle, but over time, as you cultivate forgiveness, you'll notice a significant shift in your emotional landscape. This newfound lightness allows space for compassion to emerge, not only for yourself but for others as well. Remember that forgiving others is a gift you give to yourself, freeing yourself from the chains of resentment and bitterness.

Techniques like mindfulness meditation can be enormously helpful in this process. Mindfulness allows you to become aware of your emotional state, recognizing the rise and fall of feelings without judgment. When feelings of anger or resentment arise, you can observe them without becoming entangled, allowing them to pass like clouds in the sky. This creates distance from the emotion, reducing its power to overwhelm you. Somatic practices, such as deep breathing exercises and body scans, can also be incredibly effective, helping you release physical tension associated with holding onto anger and resentment.

The integration of self-compassion, forgiveness, and acceptance is a continuous journey, not a destination. There will be moments of relapse, times when old wounds resurface. The key is to approach these moments with self-kindness, recognizing them as part of the healing process. Celebrate your progress, however small, and continue to nurture your self-compassionate nature. Remember, you deserve kindness and understanding. You are worthy of forgiveness, both from yourself and others.

Cultivating self-acceptance is intricately linked to self-compassion and forgiveness. It's about recognizing your inherent worth, regardless of your past experiences or perceived flaws. It's about accepting yourself as a whole person, embracing both your strengths and weaknesses, your light and shadow. This isn't about complacency; it's about recognizing your worthiness of love and respect, even when you make mistakes.

Self-acceptance often requires challenging negative self-talk and replacing it with self-affirmations. These affirmations are not about positive thinking in the traditional sense; they're about acknowledging your inherent value. They're about stating your worth, not as something to be earned or achieved, but as an intrinsic quality. The regular practice of self-affirmations, repeated daily, can gradually reprogram your subconscious mind, helping to replace negative self-beliefs with more positive and realistic ones.

In addition to affirmations, practicing self-care is essential for cultivating self-acceptance. Self-care encompasses a range of activities that nurture your physical, emotional, and spiritual well-being. This could include engaging in activities you enjoy, spending time in nature, prioritizing sufficient sleep, maintaining a healthy diet, or engaging in regular exercise. Prioritize activities that nourish your soul, helping you feel more grounded and centered.

Remember that self-acceptance is a process that evolves over time. It's not a destination you reach and then remain at. It's an ongoing commitment to self-compassion, self-forgiveness, and self-care. It's about embracing the totality of your being, the good, the bad, and the ugly. It's about allowing yourself to be fully human, flaws and all. And that, in itself, is a powerful act of self-love and self-acceptance. The path to healing from trauma and stress is paved with self-compassion, forgiveness, and acceptance. This journey, while challenging, is ultimately one of empowerment and profound self-discovery. It's a testament to the resilience of the human spirit and a celebration of the remarkable capacity for healing.

Chapter 4: Restoring Your Nervous System

Building upon the foundation of self-compassion, forgiveness, and self-acceptance, our journey toward healing now necessitates a deeper understanding of the physiological mechanisms underpinning our stress response. This understanding begins with the autonomic nervous system (ANS), a complex network that governs the involuntary functions of our bodies, from heartbeat and breathing to digestion and hormone release. It's the silent conductor of our internal orchestra, orchestrating the intricate dance of bodily processes without our conscious awareness. However, when faced with perceived threats, this orchestra can fall out of tune, leading to the cascade of physical and emotional symptoms we commonly associate with stress.

The ANS is broadly divided into two branches: the sympathetic nervous system (SNS) and the parasympathetic nervous system (PNS). Think of these as two counterbalancing forces, a delicate seesaw constantly adjusting to maintain internal equilibrium. The SNS, often referred to as the "fight-or-flight" system, is activated in response to perceived danger or stress. Its role is to prepare the body for immediate action, diverting resources to essential functions like muscle activation and heightened sensory awareness.

When the SNS kicks into gear, a surge of adrenaline and cortisol floods the system. Your heart races, your breathing quickens, your muscles tense, and your senses become sharper. Digestion slows, as the body prioritizes immediate survival over less crucial processes. This is a vital mechanism for handling acute threats, allowing us to react swiftly and effectively to protect ourselves. Imagine a time you narrowly avoided a car accident – the sudden surge of adrenaline, the rapid heartbeat, the heightened awareness – this is the SNS in action, ensuring your immediate safety.

However, the problem arises when the SNS remains chronically activated. In our modern world, stressors are rarely fleeting, life-threatening encounters with predators. Instead, we face prolonged periods of stress, whether from financial worries, relationship difficulties, demanding work environments, or ongoing social injustices. This sustained activation of the SNS wreaks havoc on the body, contributing to a wide range of health problems, from anxiety and depression to cardiovascular disease, autoimmune disorders, and gastrointestinal issues.

The PNS, on the other hand, is often referred to as the "rest-and-digest" system. Its role is to counteract the effects of the SNS, calming the body and promoting relaxation. When the PNS is dominant, your heart rate slows, your breathing becomes deeper and more regular, your muscles relax, and digestion resumes its normal rhythm. It's the system that fosters a sense of peace, promoting healing and restoration. Think of the feeling of contentment after a long, restful sleep, or the calm that washes over you when you're deeply engaged in a hobby you love – this is the restorative power of the PNS.

The ideal state is a balance between these two systems, a dynamic interplay that allows the body to respond appropriately to both challenges and periods of rest. However, prolonged or excessive stress can disrupt this balance, leading to a state of SNS dominance. This imbalance manifests in various ways, including chronic fatigue, sleep disturbances, digestive problems, weakened immunity, and an increased susceptibility to mental health challenges.

Understanding the interaction between the SNS and PNS is crucial for restoring nervous system health. While we can't directly control the autonomic functions of our bodies, we can influence the balance between these two systems through various interventions. Mindfulness practices, for example, have been shown to help shift the balance towards PNS dominance. By focusing on the present moment, we cultivate a sense of calm and reduce the reactivity of the SNS. Deep, slow breathing exercises directly stimulate the PNS, triggering the release of calming hormones and reducing the levels of stress hormones.

Similarly, somatic practices, which involve paying attention to and working with the body's sensations, can be extremely helpful in regulating the ANS. Yoga, tai chi, and other body-based approaches help release physical tension stored in the body, often a consequence of prolonged SNS activation. Progressive muscle relaxation, a simple yet effective technique, involves systematically tensing and releasing different muscle groups, promoting a sense of deep relaxation.

Beyond these practices, addressing the underlying stressors in your life is paramount. This may involve seeking professional support, developing healthy coping mechanisms, setting boundaries, prioritizing self-care, and fostering supportive relationships. The goal is not to eliminate stress entirely, an impossible task in our modern lives, but to develop strategies for managing stress effectively and promoting a more balanced state of nervous system regulation.

The ANS isn't merely a passive recipient of external stressors; it's a dynamic system shaped by our thoughts, beliefs, and emotions. Chronic negative thinking, for instance, can trigger a cascade of physiological responses, perpetuating a cycle of stress. Cultivating a more positive and compassionate internal dialogue can have a profound impact on the ANS, shifting the balance towards a more relaxed and resilient state. Journaling, for instance, can be a powerful tool for processing emotions, reducing their intensity, and lessening their impact on the nervous system.

Our bodies hold the memory of past traumas, storing stress in the form of physical tension. Somatic experiencing, a body-oriented approach to trauma therapy, helps individuals safely release these stored tensions, facilitating healing and restoring a sense of safety and regulation within the nervous system. This approach recognizes that trauma is not just a psychological event; it leaves a lasting imprint on the body, influencing our physical sensations, posture, and movement. By working directly with these bodily sensations, we can begin to resolve the underlying tension and restore a greater sense of equilibrium.

The journey toward restoring nervous system balance is not a quick fix; it's a process that requires patience, self-compassion, and a willingness to engage with both the emotional and physical aspects of our experiences. Just as learning to play a musical instrument takes time and practice, so too does learning to regulate our autonomic nervous system. However, the rewards are immense: increased resilience to stress, improved mental and physical health, a greater sense of inner peace, and a deeper connection to ourselves. The ability to consciously influence the balance between our SNS and PNS offers a powerful path toward healing and well-being, enhancing our capacity to navigate the challenges of life with greater ease and grace.

Our understanding of the ANS is constantly evolving, with new research continually revealing the intricate connections between the mind, body, and nervous system. This increased awareness provides a deeper understanding of the profound impact of stress on our well-being and empowers us to adopt strategies that foster a more harmonious and resilient state. By cultivating self-awareness, engaging in mindful practices, and addressing the underlying causes of stress, we can embark on a journey towards a healthier, more balanced relationship with our bodies and a life infused with greater tranquility and resilience. The integration of these practices into daily life transforms the process of healing from a passive endeavor into an active collaboration with our own innate capacity for self-regulation and restoration.

Remember that this is a journey of self-discovery and healing. There will be ups and downs, moments of progress and moments of challenge. Be patient with yourself, celebrate your victories, and approach setbacks with self-compassion and understanding. The path toward restoring your nervous system is a testament to the incredible resilience of the human spirit. With consistent effort and mindful engagement, you can cultivate a greater sense of inner peace, stability, and well-being. This deeper understanding of your own physiological responses to stress empowers you to take proactive steps towards a more balanced and fulfilling life.

We've established the crucial interplay between the sympathetic and parasympathetic nervous systems, and how chronic stress can lead to an imbalance tilting heavily towards the "fight-or-flight" response. Now, let's delve into practical techniques you can use to regain equilibrium and cultivate a more regulated nervous system. These techniques aren't merely passive exercises; they are active tools for reshaping your relationship with stress and fostering resilience. Remember, consistency is key. Start with small, manageable practices and gradually incorporate them into your daily routine.

Deep Breathing Exercises: The Foundation of Regulation

Deep, slow breathing is arguably the most accessible and potent tool for calming the nervous system. When stressed, our breathing becomes shallow and rapid, further fueling the sympathetic response. Deep breathing, conversely, activates the parasympathetic system, promoting relaxation and reducing stress hormones.

Several techniques can be employed:

Diaphragmatic Breathing (Belly Breathing): Lie down or sit comfortably with your spine straight. Place one hand on your chest and the other on your abdomen. Inhale slowly and deeply through your nose, feeling your abdomen rise as your diaphragm expands. Your chest should remain relatively still. Exhale slowly through your mouth, feeling your abdomen fall. Continue this for 5-10 minutes, focusing on the sensation of your breath entering and leaving your body. Notice the gentle rhythm, the rise and fall of your belly. If your mind wanders, gently guide it back to your breath.

Box Breathing: This technique involves inhaling for a count of four, holding for a count of four, exhaling for a count of four, and holding again for a count of four. Repeat this cycle several times. Box breathing is particularly effective in moments of acute stress, providing a quick and easy way to regain composure.

Alternate Nostril Breathing (Nadi Shodhana): This yogic technique involves alternately closing one nostril while inhaling and exhaling through the other. The gentle rhythm and focus required can be profoundly calming. There are many online tutorials demonstrating the proper technique. Beginners should start with shorter sessions and gradually increase the duration as they become more comfortable.

Remember, these are not simply exercises in breathing; they are exercises in mindful presence. Pay attention to the sensations in your body – the coolness of the air entering your nostrils, the warmth of the air leaving, the gentle expansion and contraction of your abdomen. This mindful attention shifts your focus away from anxious thoughts and allows your nervous system to relax.

Progressive Muscle Relaxation: Unwinding Physical Tension

Prolonged stress leads to chronic muscle tension, often unbeknownst to us. This tension further exacerbates the stress response, creating a vicious cycle. Progressive muscle relaxation is a powerful technique for releasing this tension and promoting deep relaxation.

The process involves systematically tensing and releasing different muscle groups. Begin by lying down comfortably.

1.

Focus on your feet: Tense the muscles in your feet by curling your toes tightly for several seconds. Notice the tension. Then, release the tension, letting your feet relax completely. Notice the difference between the tension and the release.

2.

Move up your body: Progressively tense and release the muscles in your calves, thighs, buttocks, abdomen, chest, shoulders, arms, hands, neck, and face. Pay close attention to the sensations in each muscle group. Feel the difference between tension and relaxation.

3.

Deep breathing: Incorporate deep, slow breaths during the relaxation phase of each muscle group.

4.

Visualization: Imagine the tension melting away with each exhale. Visualize a calming image or scene, such as a peaceful beach or a tranquil forest.

The entire process may take 20-30 minutes. Regular practice can significantly reduce muscle tension and improve overall relaxation. It's beneficial to use guided recordings or apps to aid in the process, particularly when first learning the technique.

Grounding Techniques: Anchoring to the Present Moment

Grounding techniques help reconnect you to the present moment, reducing feelings of anxiety and overwhelm by anchoring your awareness in your physical body and immediate surroundings.

The 5-4-3-2-1 Technique: This simple technique involves identifying five things you can see, four things you can touch, three things you can hear, two things you can smell, and one thing you can taste. This exercise shifts your attention from internal anxieties to your external environment.

Sensory Awareness: Pay attention to your physical sensations – the weight of your body on the chair, the texture of the fabric against your skin, the feeling of the air on your face. Notice any sounds in your environment – birds singing, traffic sounds, distant conversations. Engage your senses to ground yourself in the present moment.

Body Scan Meditation: A guided body scan involves systematically bringing your attention to different parts of your body, noticing any sensations without judgment. This practice increases body awareness and can help release physical tension. Many guided body scan meditations are available online or through apps.

Walking Meditation: Pay close attention to the sensation of your feet hitting the ground, the movement of your body, and the rhythm of your breath. Focus on the present moment and avoid getting caught up in your thoughts.

Mindfulness Meditation: Cultivating Present Moment Awareness

Mindfulness meditation, the practice of focusing on the present moment without judgment, has been shown to significantly reduce stress and improve nervous system regulation.

Mindful Breathing: Pay close attention to your breath without trying to change it. Notice the sensations of the breath as it enters and leaves your body. When your mind wanders, gently guide it back to your breath.

Mindful Movement: Pay attention to your body as you move, whether it's walking, stretching, or doing yoga. Notice the sensations in your muscles, joints, and breath. Appreciate the simple act of movement.

Mindful Walking: Pay attention to each step, the sensation of your feet hitting the ground, the rhythm of your breathing. Observe your surroundings without getting lost in thought.

Other Helpful Techniques:

Yoga: The combination of physical postures, breathwork, and meditation offers a holistic approach to nervous system regulation.

Tai Chi: This gentle, flowing movement practice combines meditation and martial arts, promoting relaxation and balance.

Qi Gong: Another gentle Chinese practice, involves slow movements and breathwork to cultivate energy flow and balance.

Spending time in nature: Studies have shown the restorative power of nature on the nervous system. Taking a walk in the park, sitting by a lake, or hiking in the woods can reduce stress and promote relaxation.

Listening to calming music: Select music with slow tempos and calming melodies. Classical music, ambient music, or nature sounds are often soothing.

Journaling: Writing down your thoughts and feelings can help process emotions and reduce their impact on the nervous system.

This is not an exhaustive list, but rather a starting point. Experiment with different techniques to find what works best for you. Remember that the journey to nervous system regulation is a process, not a destination. Be patient with yourself, celebrate your progress, and approach setbacks with self-compassion. With consistent practice, you can cultivate a more balanced, resilient, and peaceful relationship with your nervous system. The ability to consciously manage your stress response empowers you to live a more fulfilling and meaningful life.

Sleep is often overlooked as a fundamental pillar of health, especially when addressing trauma and stress management. However, consistent, restorative sleep is paramount for nervous system regulation and overall well-being. During sleep, our bodies and minds undertake essential repair and restorative processes. The nervous system, in particular, undergoes crucial recalibration, consolidating memories, clearing metabolic waste products, and resetting its stress response mechanisms. Insufficient or poor-quality sleep disrupts these processes, leading to a cascade of negative consequences that can significantly hinder our efforts to restore equilibrium to our nervous system.

Chronic sleep deprivation, even if it seems manageable on the surface, throws our physiological systems into a state of imbalance. Cortisol, the primary stress hormone, remains elevated, disrupting the delicate balance between our sympathetic and parasympathetic nervous systems. This persistent overactivation of the sympathetic nervous system keeps us in a perpetual state of "fight-or-flight," making us more susceptible to anxiety, irritability, and heightened emotional reactivity. Furthermore, sleep deprivation impairs our cognitive function, impacting concentration, memory, and decision-making abilities – all crucial aspects of navigating the challenges of stress and trauma recovery.

Beyond the immediate physiological effects, sleep deprivation can exacerbate pre-existing mental health conditions, such as anxiety and depression. It can also increase vulnerability to new mental health issues. Individuals struggling with trauma often experience disrupted sleep patterns, which further complicates their healing journey. The lack of restorative sleep intensifies the emotional burden of trauma, making it harder to process difficult memories and regulate emotional responses.

Therefore, establishing healthy sleep hygiene is not merely a matter of personal comfort; it's a critical component of trauma recovery and stress management. It's an active intervention, a crucial strategy to support the nervous system's natural ability to self-regulate and heal.

Improving your sleep hygiene involves adopting a multifaceted approach that addresses various factors influencing your sleep quality. This is not a one-size-fits-all solution, and experimentation to find what works best for you is key. Start by making small, incremental changes and observe their impact. Keep a sleep diary to meticulously track your sleep patterns, identifying any recurring patterns or disruptions that might be contributing to poor sleep. This data will act as your compass, guiding you toward more effective strategies.

Creating a Relaxing Bedtime Routine:

A consistent, relaxing bedtime routine signals to your body that it's time to wind down and prepare for sleep. This routine should be calming and predictable, avoiding stimulating activities right before bed. Consider incorporating the following elements:

Warm Bath or Shower: The warm water can relax muscles and promote a sense of tranquility. Adding Epsom salts can further enhance relaxation.

Gentle Stretching or Yoga: Light stretching or yoga poses can release physical tension and prepare your body for rest. Avoid strenuous exercise close to bedtime.

Mindful Meditation or Deep Breathing Exercises: Practice techniques already discussed in this chapter, using deep breathing, progressive muscle relaxation, or mindfulness meditation to quiet the mind and reduce stress hormone levels.

Reading a Book: Choose a calming book; avoid screens for at least an hour before bed. The gentle rhythm of reading can promote relaxation and prepare you for sleep.

Listening to Calming Music: Select music with slow tempos and calming melodies. Avoid music with strong rhythms or lyrics that may stimulate your mind.

Journaling: Writing down your thoughts and feelings can help process emotions and reduce their intensity, creating a sense of mental clarity before sleep.

Aromatherapy: Certain scents, such as lavender or chamomile, can promote relaxation. Use a diffuser or add a few drops of essential oil to your bathwater.

The key is consistency. Establish a regular bedtime and wake-up time, even on weekends, to regulate your body's natural sleep-wake cycle. Aim for seven to nine hours of sleep each night.

Optimizing Your Sleep Environment:

Your sleep environment significantly influences sleep quality. Creating a conducive sleep space is crucial for promoting restorative sleep.

Darkness: Darkness signals to your body that it's time to sleep. Make sure your bedroom is dark, using blackout curtains if necessary. Consider using an eye mask if light from outside or from electronic devices interferes with your sleep.

Quiet: Minimize noise disturbances as much as possible. Use earplugs if necessary, or consider a white noise machine to mask disruptive sounds.

Cool Temperature: A slightly cool room temperature is ideal for sleep. Most people sleep best in a room temperature between 60-67°F (15-19°C).

Comfortable Bedding: Invest in comfortable bedding that supports your body and helps regulate your temperature. Consider using high-quality sheets, pillows, and a mattress that meets your individual needs.

Cleanliness and Order: A clean and organized bedroom creates a sense of calm and tranquility, which is conducive to sleep.

Ventilation: Ensure adequate ventilation in your bedroom to maintain fresh air circulation.

Understanding Sleep Debt:

Sleep debt refers to the cumulative effect of insufficient sleep over time. It's not just about missing a night's sleep; it's about the chronic deficit that accumulates over weeks, months, or even years. This cumulative sleep deficit negatively affects mood, cognition, and physical health. It's crucial to understand that consistently sleeping less than your required amount leaves you in a perpetual state of sleep debt.

Addressing sleep debt is not a quick fix. It requires a gradual and sustained effort to prioritize sleep and address any underlying sleep disturbances. Gradually increasing your sleep duration by 15-30 minutes each night can help you slowly repay your sleep debt. This gradual approach allows your body to adjust without experiencing adverse effects. If you're struggling to repay your sleep debt, consider seeking professional help from a sleep specialist or healthcare provider.

Tracking Your Sleep:

Keeping a sleep diary is incredibly valuable for understanding your sleep patterns and identifying areas for improvement. This diary should include information such as:

Bedtime and wake-up time: Record your bedtime and wake-up time each day.

Sleep duration: Calculate the total number of hours you slept.

Sleep quality: Rate your sleep quality on a scale of 1 to 10, with 10 being the best sleep.

Any disturbances: Note any events or factors that may have disrupted your sleep, such as noise, light, or stress.

Daytime sleepiness: Record how sleepy or alert you felt throughout the day.

Caffeine and alcohol consumption: Note your caffeine and alcohol intake, as these substances can significantly impact sleep quality.

Physical activity: Record any physical activities you engaged in during the day.

By consistently tracking your sleep, you'll gain valuable insights into your sleep patterns, allowing you to fine-tune your sleep hygiene strategies and improve your sleep quality over time. Remember, consistent, restorative sleep is an indispensable component of trauma recovery and stress management, actively supporting your nervous system's capacity for self-regulation and healing. Prioritizing sleep is an act of self-care, a fundamental step in building resilience and fostering overall well-being.

Nourishing your body through mindful eating and consistent physical activity is crucial for supporting nervous system regulation and overall well-being, particularly when recovering from trauma or managing chronic stress. These two pillars of health work synergistically; proper nutrition fuels your body's ability to engage in physical activity, and physical activity, in turn, enhances nutrient absorption and metabolism. Both contribute significantly to reducing stress hormones, improving sleep quality, and boosting the production of neurotransmitters crucial for emotional regulation and resilience. Let's delve deeper into how we can optimize both nutrition and physical activity for optimal nervous system health.

Building a Foundation of Nourishment:

The food we consume directly impacts our brain chemistry and nervous system function. A diet rich in whole, unprocessed foods provides the essential building blocks for neurotransmitter synthesis and cellular repair. Conversely, a diet high in processed foods, sugar, and unhealthy fats can disrupt hormonal balance, leading to increased inflammation and exacerbating symptoms of stress and anxiety.

Think of your body as a complex machine. To perform optimally, it needs the right fuel. This fuel comes in the form of a balanced diet that incorporates the following key components:

Complex Carbohydrates: These are your slow-release energy sources, providing sustained energy throughout the day and avoiding the blood sugar crashes associated with simple sugars. Excellent sources include whole grains like brown rice, quinoa, oats, and whole-wheat bread. Legumes such as lentils, chickpeas, and beans are also excellent sources of complex carbohydrates, along with providing fiber and essential proteins. Incorporating these into your diet offers a more stable energy source, reducing the likelihood of experiencing energy dips that can trigger stress and anxiety.

Lean Proteins: Proteins are the building blocks of our cells, including neurotransmitters. Opt for lean sources such as fish (rich in omega-3 fatty acids), poultry, beans, lentils, and tofu. Adequate protein intake supports the repair and regeneration of nerve cells, particularly crucial after experiencing trauma. A deficiency in protein can impair neurotransmitter production, potentially leading to mood imbalances and heightened stress responses.

Healthy Fats: Essential fatty acids, particularly omega-3s, are critical for brain health and nervous system function. They are involved in reducing inflammation, improving mood, and supporting cognitive function. Excellent sources include fatty fish like salmon, mackerel, and tuna;

flaxseeds; chia seeds; and walnuts. Aim for a balance of omega-3 and omega-6 fatty acids, as an imbalance can contribute to inflammation.

Fruits and Vegetables: These are packed with vitamins, minerals, and antioxidants, providing essential nutrients that support overall health and cellular function. They're not only beneficial for digestion but also contribute to reducing inflammation throughout the body, thereby benefiting nervous system health. Aim for a variety of colorful fruits and vegetables to ensure you're getting a wide range of nutrients.

Hydration: Water is often overlooked but is absolutely crucial for all bodily functions, including nervous system regulation. Dehydration can lead to fatigue, headaches, and impair cognitive function, making it harder to manage stress. Aim to drink plenty of water throughout the day.

Beyond simply choosing healthy foods, paying attention to

how you eat is equally important. Mindful eating involves savoring each bite, paying attention to the flavors and textures of your food, and eating without distractions such as television or electronic devices. This practice can enhance digestion, improve nutrient absorption, and foster a more positive relationship with food, contributing to overall well-being. Avoid rushed meals, and take time to fully appreciate your food.

Addressing Specific Nutritional Needs:

Individuals recovering from trauma may have specific nutritional needs based on their unique circumstances and experiences. For instance, some may experience digestive issues that require a more tailored approach. Consulting a registered dietitian or nutritionist specialized in trauma-informed care can be incredibly beneficial. They can help identify specific nutritional deficiencies, create personalized dietary plans that address individual needs, and help manage any digestive issues that may arise from stress or trauma. They may suggest supplements like magnesium, Vitamin D, or probiotics to support overall health and nervous system function based on your individual requirements.

Integrating Movement into Your Routine:

Regular physical activity is not just about physical fitness; it's a potent tool for stress management and nervous system regulation. Exercise promotes the release of endorphins, natural mood boosters that combat stress and anxiety. It also improves sleep quality, boosts cognitive function, and enhances overall resilience.

The key is finding activities you enjoy and can sustain. There's no one-size-fits-all approach; experimentation is essential. Consider incorporating the following types of physical activity:

Aerobic Exercise: Activities such as walking, running, swimming, cycling, or dancing elevate your heart rate and improve cardiovascular health. These activities are particularly effective for stress reduction and improving mood. Aim for at least 150 minutes of moderate-intensity aerobic activity or 75 minutes of vigorous-intensity aerobic activity per week.

Strength Training: Incorporating strength training exercises two or three times per week builds muscle mass, improves bone density, and increases overall strength. This can enhance self-confidence and improve body image, which are significant factors in trauma recovery. Focus on compound exercises that work multiple muscle groups simultaneously.

Yoga and Pilates: These practices combine physical movement with mindfulness and deep breathing, providing a powerful combination for stress reduction and nervous system regulation. Yoga and Pilates can improve flexibility, increase body awareness, and promote relaxation.

Mindful Movement: Even simple activities like walking in nature, gardening, or stretching can be incredibly beneficial for both physical and mental health. Pay attention to your body as you move, focusing on your breath and the sensations in your body. This mindful approach can help reduce stress and enhance body awareness.

The intensity and duration of your physical activity should be tailored to your individual fitness level and preferences. Begin gradually and avoid pushing yourself too hard, especially if you're just starting. Listen to your body and rest when needed. Remember that consistency is key; even short bursts of activity throughout the day can be more effective than one long, strenuous workout.

The Synergy of Nutrition and Movement:

Nutrition and physical activity are deeply interconnected. Proper nutrition fuels your body for physical activity, while exercise enhances nutrient absorption and metabolism. This synergistic relationship is essential for optimal nervous system function and overall well-being. Combining a healthy diet with regular physical activity can significantly reduce stress hormones, improve sleep quality, and boost the production of neurotransmitters that are crucial for emotional regulation and resilience. Prioritizing both nutrition and physical activity is an act of self-care, a crucial step in building resilience and fostering overall well-being, particularly during and after the trauma recovery process. Remember to be patient with yourself, celebrate small victories, and remember that consistency is more important than intensity. The journey toward restoring your nervous system is a marathon, not a sprint.

Creating a personalized daily self-care routine is a crucial step in restoring your nervous system's equilibrium and fostering overall well-being. This isn't about adding more tasks to your already full plate; rather, it's about consciously incorporating practices that nourish your mind, body, and spirit, providing the support your nervous system needs to heal and thrive. The key lies in identifying your unique needs and preferences, and building a routine that feels sustainable and genuinely supportive, not burdensome.

The first step is self-reflection. Take some time to consider what truly nourishes you. What activities make you feel calm, centered, and energized? What brings you joy, reduces stress, and helps you connect with yourself? Consider your physical, emotional, and spiritual needs. Do you crave moments of quiet solitude or thrive in social connection? Do you need vigorous movement or gentle stretches? The answers are deeply personal, and there are no right or wrong answers.

To help you explore these questions, consider journaling. Spend some time each day, even just five to ten minutes, reflecting on your experiences, feelings, and needs. Ask yourself:

What activities bring me a sense of peace and calm?

What helps me manage stress effectively?

What makes me feel connected to myself and others?

What aspects of my well-being are currently neglected?

What small acts of self-compassion can I incorporate into my daily routine?

These prompts can help you identify areas you might want to focus on in your self-care routine. Your answers may change over time, and that's perfectly acceptable. Self-care is an evolving process, not a static destination.

Once you have a clearer understanding of your needs, start by incorporating small, manageable practices into your daily routine. These could include:

Mindful Moments: Start with short periods of mindfulness, even just five minutes a day. Focus on your breath, noticing the sensation of the air entering and leaving your body. Pay attention to the subtle shifts in your body and mind without judgment. Apps like Calm or Headspace can offer guided meditations if you find it challenging to begin independently. You might choose to practice mindfulness during your morning coffee, while waiting for a bus, or during your lunch break. These small moments of presence can accumulate, significantly reducing stress and improving your overall sense of well-being.

Gentle Movement: Incorporate gentle movement into your day, even if you aren't a fitness enthusiast. A short walk in nature, some gentle stretching, or a few minutes of yoga can be incredibly beneficial. The goal is not to exhaust yourself, but to gently move your body, increase blood flow, and release endorphins. Consider trying chair yoga if mobility is a concern, or simply taking the stairs instead of the elevator.

Connecting with Nature: Spending time in nature has been shown to have a profoundly positive effect on mental and emotional well-being. Even a few minutes spent observing the natural world can reduce stress hormones and promote relaxation. Take a walk in a park, sit by a tree, or simply look out of a window and appreciate the natural beauty around you. The sights, sounds, and smells of nature can have a restorative effect on your nervous system.

Creative Expression: Engage in creative activities that bring you joy. This could be anything from painting and drawing to writing, playing music, or knitting. Creative expression provides a healthy outlet for emotions, reduces stress, and fosters self-discovery. Don't worry about being perfect or producing a masterpiece; the focus is on the process and the enjoyment of the experience.

Connecting with Loved Ones: Social connection is essential for well-being. Spend time with people who make you feel supported, loved, and understood. This might involve a phone call with a friend, a coffee date with a colleague, or a family gathering. Human connection is essential for a thriving nervous system.

Prioritizing Sleep: Adequate sleep is crucial for nervous system regulation. Aim for seven to nine hours of quality sleep each night. Create a relaxing bedtime routine to help you unwind before bed. This could involve a warm bath, reading a book, or listening to calming music. Minimize screen time in the hour leading up to bed. A consistent sleep schedule can enhance the quality of your rest, allowing your body to engage in restorative processes.

Digital Detox: Take regular breaks from electronic devices. Constant exposure to screens can lead to increased stress, anxiety, and sleep disturbances. Schedule specific times to disconnect and engage in activities that are screen-free. This could be as simple as setting a time each day to put away your phone, or completely powering down your devices during a specific time each day.

Mindful Eating: Practice mindful eating, savoring each bite and paying attention to the flavors and textures of your food. Avoid eating while distracted by screens or other activities. This mindful approach can improve digestion, reduce stress, and enhance your overall relationship with food.

Setting Boundaries: Learn to set healthy boundaries with others. This involves saying no to requests that drain your energy or compromise your well-being. Establishing boundaries is an act of self-respect and is essential for reducing stress and protecting your mental health. Being able to say no, without guilt or self-blame, is an essential component of stress management.

Self-Compassion: Treat yourself with the same kindness and understanding that you would offer a close friend. Practice self-forgiveness when you make mistakes, and acknowledge your strengths and accomplishments. Self-compassion is a powerful tool for building resilience and promoting emotional well-being.

Building a self-care routine is a process, not a destination. Start with one or two practices that resonate with you and gradually add more as you feel comfortable. Don't strive for perfection; aim for consistency. Even small acts of self-care can make a significant difference in your overall well-being. Remember to listen to your body and adjust your routine as needed. What works for you today may not work for you tomorrow, and that's okay. The flexibility to adapt your routine as your needs evolve is part of the process.

It's important to note that creating a self-care routine is not a quick fix for deep-seated trauma. If you are struggling with the impacts of trauma, it's crucial to seek professional help from a therapist or counselor specializing in trauma-informed care. They can provide you with additional support and guidance, helping you process your experiences and develop healthy coping mechanisms. A self-care routine is a complement to professional support, not a replacement.

Consider keeping a self-care journal to track your progress and identify what practices are most effective for you. Note down the activities you've engaged in, how they made you feel, and any adjustments you need to make. Reflecting on your experience can help you refine your routine and maximize its effectiveness. Remember, the ultimate goal is to create a routine that supports your overall well-being and empowers you to navigate life's challenges with greater resilience and self-compassion. This is a journey of self-discovery, and embracing the process with patience and self-compassion is key to long-term success. Celebrate small victories along the way; every step you take towards prioritizing your well-being is a significant achievement.

Chapter 5: Setting Healthy Boundaries

Setting healthy boundaries is not merely a desirable trait; it's a fundamental necessity for emotional and mental well-being, especially for individuals navigating the aftermath of trauma. Boundaries act as protective shields, safeguarding our energy, time, and emotional resources from being depleted by others' needs or demands. They are the invisible lines we draw to define what we are willing to accept and what we will not tolerate in our relationships and interactions. Without these boundaries, we risk becoming overwhelmed, resentful, and even experiencing a relapse into past trauma patterns.

Understanding the importance of boundaries requires acknowledging their multifaceted role in our lives. They're not about being selfish or uncaring; rather, they're about self-respect and self-preservation. They allow us to maintain a sense of autonomy and control, crucial for individuals who may have experienced a loss of control in the past. Think of your boundaries as the guardians of your emotional and mental health, protecting you from situations that could trigger distress or exacerbate existing vulnerabilities.

For those who have experienced trauma, establishing healthy boundaries can feel particularly challenging. Trauma often leaves individuals with a distorted sense of self and their relationships with others. This can manifest as people-pleasing behaviors, a reluctance to assert one's needs, and a pervasive fear of conflict. These behaviors, while seemingly rooted in kindness or a desire to avoid conflict, often stem from a deeply ingrained need to control or prevent any potential threat or abandonment, learned as a coping mechanism in earlier trauma. The fear of upsetting someone, triggering conflict, or causing others pain can be so significant that it overrides personal needs and desires.

Consider the impact of past experiences. If you grew up in an environment where your feelings were disregarded, your needs unmet, or your boundaries constantly violated, the ability to set and maintain boundaries may feel unnatural or even frightening. The ingrained habit of suppressing your needs to placate others becomes automatic, almost unconscious. This leads to a chronic state of emotional exhaustion, impacting self-esteem, perpetuating patterns of unhealthy relationships, and hindering personal growth. It is only by consciously unlearning these maladaptive coping mechanisms and developing new, healthier strategies that you can begin to set boundaries effectively.

The process of setting boundaries requires self-awareness, assertiveness, and a willingness to challenge long-held beliefs and patterns. The first step involves recognizing your own personal needs and limits. What activities drain your energy? What types of interactions leave you feeling emotionally depleted? What are your non-negotiables—those aspects of your life that you refuse to compromise? This self-reflection is crucial for defining your boundaries.

Journaling can be an invaluable tool in this process. By writing down your experiences, your feelings, and your observations, you gain a clearer understanding of your emotional responses to various situations and relationships. Identify recurrent patterns. Are you consistently saying "yes" when you really want to say "no"? Are you sacrificing your needs for the sake of others, leaving yourself feeling resentful and overwhelmed? Analyzing these patterns offers insights into your current boundaries and their effectiveness.

Once you have a clear sense of your limits, you can begin to assert your boundaries in a healthy and constructive way. This doesn't involve being aggressive or confrontational; it's about expressing your needs clearly and respectfully. Effective communication is paramount. Learn to use "I" statements to convey your feelings and needs without blaming or accusing others. For example, instead of saying, "You always make me feel pressured," try saying, "I feel overwhelmed when there are too many demands on my time, and I need to prioritize my needs."

Setting boundaries can be emotionally taxing initially, especially if you are not accustomed to doing so. You might anticipate resistance or conflict, provoking anxiety. You may feel guilt or self-doubt, believing that you're being selfish or inconsiderate. These are entirely normal reactions, reflecting the ingrained patterns you are actively unlearning. Remember that your need for self-preservation is valid and important. Prioritizing your well-being is not selfish; it's self-care.

It's essential to practice self-compassion during this process. Treat yourself with the same kindness and understanding that you would offer a close friend navigating a similar challenge. Acknowledge the effort you are making and celebrate your small victories. Each time you successfully assert a boundary, you are reinforcing a new, healthier pattern of behavior, gradually replacing old, unhealthy coping mechanisms.

Setting boundaries isn't a one-time event but rather an ongoing process that requires consistent practice and refinement. You will likely encounter situations where your boundaries are tested. This is an opportunity for learning and growth. Don't be discouraged by setbacks; instead, view them as opportunities to reinforce your boundaries and improve your communication skills.

The benefits of setting healthy boundaries extend far beyond protecting your emotional well-being. By setting clear limits, you improve the quality of your relationships. Healthy boundaries foster respect and mutual understanding, allowing for more authentic and fulfilling connections. When you establish clear boundaries, you create space for genuine reciprocity, strengthening the bonds you value while protecting yourself from those that are detrimental. Relationships become less about pleasing others and more about mutually supportive interactions.

Furthermore, setting boundaries enhances self-esteem. By prioritizing your needs and asserting yourself, you cultivate a sense of self-respect and confidence. It helps you reclaim your sense of autonomy and control over your life, reducing the feeling of powerlessness that can be particularly acute following trauma. This self-assuredness empowers you to navigate life's challenges with greater resilience and emotional fortitude.

The journey towards establishing healthy boundaries is deeply personal. There is no single "right" way to do it. Experiment with different approaches until you find what works best for you. Be patient with yourself and celebrate your successes. Remember that you deserve to be respected, protected, and empowered. The process of setting boundaries is an act of self-love, an affirmation of your own inherent worth and value. With consistent practice and self-compassion, you can create the protective space you need to heal, thrive, and build a life based on respect, self-care, and genuine connection. Seeking professional guidance from a therapist or counselor can provide invaluable support throughout this process, especially if you are struggling with the emotional challenges associated with trauma. They can offer personalized strategies, coping mechanisms, and the support you need to navigate this important journey. Remember that this is a journey of self-discovery and empowerment, one step at a time.

Identifying boundary violations can be surprisingly complex. It's not always a dramatic event; often, the erosion of boundaries happens subtly, almost imperceptibly, over time. Recognizing these violations is crucial for reclaiming your sense of self and establishing healthier relationships. This involves understanding the nuances of healthy boundaries and recognizing the subtle ways in which they can be transgressed.

One of the most common challenges in identifying boundary violations is the internalization of societal norms that normalize or even encourage boundary crossing. We're often taught to be accommodating, to put others' needs before our own, and to avoid conflict at all costs. This societal pressure can make it difficult to recognize when our own boundaries are being violated because we may have been conditioned to accept such behaviors as normal or even expected. For instance, feeling obligated to work overtime even when it interferes with personal commitments or saying "yes" to requests that deplete your energy are examples of this normalized boundary crossing. The constant pressure to be available, responsive, and agreeable can lead to chronic exhaustion and resentment, silently eroding your well-being.

Furthermore, the aftermath of trauma can significantly complicate the recognition of boundary violations. Individuals who have experienced trauma may have a diminished sense of self-worth and a heightened sensitivity to perceived threats. This can lead to a tendency to minimize or ignore boundary violations, rationalizing them as unavoidable or even deserved. The fear of conflict or abandonment, deeply rooted in past experiences, can override the instinct to protect oneself. For example, a survivor of domestic violence might tolerate controlling behavior from a partner, attributing it to their own flaws or fearing the consequences of leaving. Or, someone who experienced emotional neglect in childhood might accept overly demanding friendships, feeling unworthy of healthier boundaries.

To effectively identify boundary violations, it's crucial to become acutely aware of your own emotional and physical responses. Pay attention to your feelings and physical sensations in different situations and interactions. Do you feel drained, anxious, or resentful after spending time with certain individuals or engaging in specific activities? Does your body tense up, your stomach churn, or your heart race when someone makes a certain request? These physical and emotional signals are often early warning systems indicating that your boundaries are being pushed or crossed.

Boundary violations can manifest in a wide range of ways, depending on the relationship and context. In close relationships, these violations can be subtle and pervasive. A partner consistently dismissing your feelings, making decisions without your input, or criticizing you relentlessly is a significant boundary violation. Similarly, a friend who constantly borrows money without repaying it, monopolizes conversations, or frequently cancels plans at the last minute is demonstrating a lack of respect for your time, resources, and emotional well-being. Family dynamics can also present challenges, with overbearing or intrusive family members crossing boundaries by giving unsolicited advice, sharing personal information without consent, or making demands that overshadow your own needs.

In professional settings, boundary violations might involve unreasonable workload demands, harassment or bullying, or a lack of respect for your personal time. A boss who consistently sends emails late at night, expects you to work through weekends without compensation, or belittles your contributions in meetings is clearly overstepping professional boundaries. Similarly, colleagues who gossip about you, make inappropriate comments, or undermine your work are creating a hostile and disrespectful environment. These violations not only impact your mental and emotional health but can also significantly hinder your career progression and job satisfaction.

Beyond these specific examples, there are more subtle forms of boundary violations that are often easily missed. These might include subtle forms of coercion, such as guilt-tripping or manipulation. For example, someone might say, "If you really loved me, you would..." to coerce you into doing something you don't want to do. Another subtle violation might be unsolicited advice or opinions given without asking for it. While well-intentioned, these actions can still feel invasive and disrespectful, especially if the advice is unwelcome or unsolicited. Passive-aggressive behaviors, such as ignoring your requests or responding with sarcasm, are also forms of boundary violations that can be difficult to address directly.

Identifying past experiences of boundary violations is a crucial step in healing and establishing healthier patterns. Take some time to reflect on your past relationships, both personal and professional. Consider instances where you felt pressured, manipulated, or disrespected. Remember situations where you felt a sense of unease, anxiety, or resentment, even if you didn't explicitly recognize them as boundary violations at the time. Journaling can be an invaluable tool in this process; by writing down your experiences, you create a space for self-reflection and gain a deeper understanding of your past experiences and how they shape your current boundaries.

This reflection is not about assigning blame or dwelling on past hurts, but about recognizing patterns of behavior and identifying recurring themes. Were your boundaries consistently violated in certain relationships? Did you frequently find yourself compromising your needs to avoid conflict or maintain harmony? By acknowledging these patterns, you gain valuable insight into your current behaviors and can start to identify the triggers that may lead to future boundary violations.

Consider the various aspects of your life – your family relationships, romantic relationships, friendships, and professional interactions. Within each of these areas, reflect on specific instances where you felt your boundaries were disregarded, and then analyze these experiences in detail. Ask yourself the following: What happened? How did you feel physically and emotionally? Did you assert yourself or did you acquiesce? What were the consequences? What could you have done differently? These questions will help illuminate the pattern of boundary violations in your life.

It's essential to remember that identifying boundary violations is not about fault-finding; it's about self-awareness and self-protection. It's about understanding your needs and establishing the parameters that maintain your well-being. By recognizing past violations, you can develop stronger boundaries in the future. This increased awareness empowers you to make informed choices, fostering healthier relationships and promoting a greater sense of self-respect and autonomy. This process of self-discovery is a powerful step towards reclaiming your agency and building a life rooted in emotional safety and self-preservation. It's a crucial step toward not only healing from past traumas but also toward fostering fulfilling and healthy relationships in the future. Remembering that recognizing these violations is a vital part of the journey towards establishing healthy boundaries, you take a critical step towards creating a healthier and more fulfilling life for yourself. The process is gradual, and self-compassion is essential, allowing you to learn from past experiences without judgment, fostering growth and strength.

Building upon our exploration of identifying boundary violations, we now turn to the crucial skill of assertive communication—the cornerstone of maintaining healthy boundaries. Assertiveness is not about aggression or passivity; it's about expressing your needs and opinions respectfully and directly, without infringing on the rights of others. It's a delicate balance, requiring both self-respect and consideration for others. Mastering assertive communication allows you to clearly articulate your boundaries while navigating interpersonal dynamics with grace and confidence.

One of the fundamental aspects of assertive communication is clarity. Avoid ambiguous language or hinting at your needs. Instead, use "I" statements to express your feelings and desires without blaming or accusing others. For example, instead of saying, "You always interrupt me," try, "I feel unheard when I'm interrupted. Could we please allow each other to finish our thoughts?" This subtle shift in phrasing transforms a potentially accusatory statement into a respectful request for consideration. Remember, the goal is not to win an argument, but to create understanding and cooperation.

Direct communication is another essential element of assertiveness. Avoid passive-aggressive behaviors, such as sarcasm or silent treatment, which often lead to miscommunication and resentment. Instead, address issues directly and honestly, expressing your needs and concerns clearly and concisely. This direct approach prevents misunderstandings and allows for open dialogue, fostering a healthier and more transparent relationship. Consider the scenario where a colleague consistently borrows your supplies without asking. Instead of simmering in resentment, directly address the issue: "I've noticed my [supplies] have been missing lately. I would appreciate it if you'd ask before borrowing them in the future." This direct yet respectful approach avoids passive aggression and establishes clear expectations.

Active listening is an equally important aspect of assertive communication. Truly hearing and understanding the other person's perspective, even if you disagree, shows respect and creates a foundation for productive dialogue. When engaging in a conversation about boundaries, actively listen to what the other person is saying, ask clarifying questions, and summarize their points to ensure understanding. This demonstrates that you value their perspective and are committed to finding a mutually acceptable solution. Active listening goes beyond merely hearing words; it involves observing body language, recognizing emotional cues, and reflecting back the essence of what the other person is communicating. For instance, if someone expresses frustration about your boundary, acknowledge their feelings: "I hear your frustration about not being able to [action], and I want to find a way that works for both of us."

To further refine your assertive communication skills, consider practicing role-playing exercises. These exercises can be immensely beneficial in preparing for real-life situations. A trusted friend or therapist can help you practice expressing your needs in different scenarios, allowing you to hone your skills in a safe and supportive environment. You can practice various scenarios, such as setting boundaries with family members, colleagues, or friends, ensuring you feel confident and prepared to assert your needs in diverse contexts. The goal is to develop flexibility and adaptability in your approach, creating a range of assertive responses that can be utilized based on the situation and relationship dynamic.

Consider the following example: Imagine you're consistently asked to work late despite having prior commitments. You might practice a response such as, "I appreciate the extra work, but I've already made plans for the evening. I'm not available to work late tonight, but I can dedicate time tomorrow morning to catch up." This assertive statement clearly communicates your unavailability while offering a viable alternative, preventing resentment and maintaining a professional relationship.

Nonverbal communication plays a critical role in assertive communication. Maintaining eye contact, using a calm and steady tone of voice, and employing open body language conveys confidence and self-assurance. Avoid fidgeting or shrinking back, as these nonverbal cues might inadvertently undermine your message. A confident stance, steady eye contact, and a clear, calm tone of voice significantly influence how your message is perceived. Consider the impact of posture; an upright posture conveys confidence and assertiveness, whereas slouching might project insecurity. Practice in front of a mirror; observe your body language, and refine your non-verbal communication techniques.

Empathy, while essential, should not override the assertion of your boundaries. While understanding the other person's perspective is important, it's crucial to maintain your sense of self and prioritize your needs. Empathy allows for understanding, but assertiveness ensures your needs are met. It's not about dismissing their concerns, but about finding a solution that respects both parties' boundaries. For example, if a friend continually relies on you for emotional support to the detriment of your well-being, empathetically expressing your limits is key. You might say, "I care about you and want to support you, but I'm feeling overwhelmed by the constant demands on my time and energy. I need to set some boundaries to protect my mental health. Perhaps we can schedule regular check-ins to maintain our friendship without exhausting me."

It's important to remember that assertiveness is a skill, not a personality trait. It's something that can be learned and improved upon with practice. Start by identifying small situations where you can practice assertive communication. This might involve setting simple boundaries, such as saying "no" to a request you don't feel comfortable with or politely refusing an invitation. Each small success builds confidence, empowering you to tackle more challenging situations. Start by saying no to trivial requests, and gradually increase the level of difficulty. The more you practice, the more natural and effortless assertive communication will become.

Dealing with potential pushback or resistance is an inevitable part of setting boundaries. Some individuals may initially resist your attempts to establish clearer boundaries, testing your resolve. Maintain your composure and reiterate your needs clearly and calmly, avoiding getting into an argument. Remember, the goal is to establish boundaries, not to "win" a dispute. If resistance persists despite your best efforts, consider seeking support from a trusted friend, family member, or therapist. They can provide guidance and emotional support as you navigate the complexities of setting boundaries and maintaining them in the face of resistance.

Building resilience to pushback involves anticipating potential objections and formulating strategies to address them. Understanding why someone might resist your boundaries is the first step; it enables you to tailor your communication effectively. Often, resistance stems from fear of change, dependence, or misunderstanding. Addressing these concerns directly and calmly helps de-escalate conflict and fosters understanding. For example, if a family member resists your new boundaries, calmly explain the reasons behind them and how these changes are beneficial for both of you. Empathetically address their concerns and demonstrate a willingness to collaborate on finding a balanced solution. For instance, if a family member criticizes your newly established limits, you might say, "I understand you're concerned about [their concern], and I want to assure you this is not about rejecting you, but about prioritizing my well-being. Let's find a way to maintain our relationship while respecting my need for space."

Remember, setting healthy boundaries is a continuous process, not a one-time event. It requires consistent self-reflection, adjustments, and practice. There will be times when your boundaries are challenged, and you'll need to reassert them. Be patient with yourself; it takes time to develop and maintain assertive communication and healthy boundaries. Celebrate your successes and learn from any setbacks. This journey towards self-respect and healthier relationships is a lifelong commitment that will bring considerable rewards in terms of well-being and fulfilling connections. This ongoing process emphasizes the importance of self-compassion and patience in establishing and maintaining healthy boundaries, fostering resilience in the face of challenges and promoting personal growth. The journey is unique to each individual and requires mindful attention and sustained effort.

Saying no often feels like navigating a minefield, especially for those accustomed to prioritizing others' needs above their own. This tendency, frequently rooted in past experiences of trauma or learned people-pleasing behaviors, can leave individuals feeling depleted, resentful, and overwhelmed. The discomfort associated with refusal isn't merely social awkwardness; it can be a deep-seated fear stemming from past experiences where asserting oneself led to negative consequences – punishment, rejection, or emotional distress. Understanding this underlying fear is crucial to dismantling the guilt that often accompanies saying no.

The first step towards overcoming this guilt is recognizing and challenging the underlying beliefs fueling it. Many people carry deeply ingrained beliefs about their worth and their role in relationships. These beliefs might include: "I'm not important enough to say no," "Saying no will make people angry or dislike me," "My value lies in my willingness to help others, regardless of my own needs," or "If I say no, I'll be a bad [parent/friend/employee/partner]." These are often deeply ingrained, unconscious beliefs that need to be brought to light and challenged. Journaling can be a valuable tool here; by writing down these beliefs, you can begin to examine them critically and question their validity.

Cognitive reframing is a powerful technique to address these limiting beliefs. It involves identifying the negative thought pattern ("Saying no will make them angry") and replacing it with a more realistic and balanced one ("Saying no is a way of protecting my well-being and it doesn't necessarily mean they will be angry; it may even improve our relationship in the long run"). This process may require significant self-reflection and potentially the guidance of a therapist to identify the root of these beliefs and replace them with healthier, more self-affirming ones. Remember that these beliefs are not facts; they are interpretations of past experiences, and these interpretations can be revised.

Another crucial aspect is understanding the difference between assertive refusal and aggressive rejection. Assertiveness involves clearly expressing your needs and boundaries without being aggressive or hostile. Aggression involves attacking or belittling the other person, often resulting in conflict and damaged relationships. Passive behavior, on the other hand, avoids direct communication and often results in suppressed resentment. Assertiveness occupies the middle ground, allowing you to prioritize your own needs while maintaining respect for others. The key is to find a balance between your needs and theirs, recognizing that your needs are valid and deserving of consideration.

Practicing assertive refusals starts with small steps. Begin by saying no to minor requests – declining an extra task at work that would encroach on your lunch break, turning down a social invitation that you don't genuinely want to attend. Each successful "no" builds confidence and reduces the fear associated with refusal. Start with situations that hold minimal personal risk, building a foundation of successful assertions before tackling more challenging scenarios. The goal is not to become a hermit, but to learn to navigate requests respectfully while protecting your own time, energy, and mental health.

When saying no, framing your refusal is essential. Using "I" statements is vital in fostering understanding and preventing the other person from feeling attacked. Instead of saying "You always ask me to do this," try "I'm not able to do this right now due to prior commitments." Avoid making excuses, as they often undermine your assertion and can lead to further requests. Direct and honest communication is key; be clear and concise about your unavailability or unwillingness.

The phrasing you use significantly impacts the reception of your refusal. Consider the following examples:

Instead of: "I can't help you with that." (Sounds dismissive)

Try: "I'm unable to assist with that at this time due to my current workload." (More informative and less dismissive)

Instead of: "That's not my problem." (Rude and dismissive)

Try: "I understand you're facing a challenge, but I'm not the best resource to address this particular issue. Perhaps [alternative solution or person] would be able to assist you." (Offers a helpful alternative)

Instead of: "No way!" (Abrupt and unsympathetic)

Try: "I appreciate you thinking of me, but I won't be able to assist with this right now." (Polite and respectful)

Preparation is key. If you anticipate a request you might refuse, consider rehearsing your response beforehand. This mental preparation reduces anxiety and allows you to respond calmly and confidently when the moment arises. This mental rehearsal can be especially helpful in high-stakes situations where the consequences of refusal might feel significant.

Anticipating pushback is also critical. Some individuals may react negatively to your refusal, attempting to guilt-trip, manipulate, or pressure you into compliance. Having prepared responses for these situations is essential. You might respond with something like: "I understand you're disappointed, but my decision is firm. I appreciate your understanding." Or, "While I value our relationship, I need to prioritize my own well-being. My response remains the same." It's important to hold your ground while maintaining respect and empathy for the other person's feelings. It's not about hurting their feelings; it's about setting healthy boundaries for yourself.

Furthermore, recognize that not everyone will react positively to your boundaries. Some individuals might attempt to manipulate or guilt you into changing your mind. Setting boundaries often reveals the dynamics of your relationships, exposing unhealthy patterns or power imbalances. This might be uncomfortable, but it also presents an opportunity for growth and healthier relationships. It's not about changing the other person; it's about changing how you engage with them and the boundaries you allow in the relationship.

In some cases, saying no might necessitate a renegotiation of expectations within a relationship. This can involve open and honest communication about your limitations and how you can better contribute while protecting your own well-being. It might involve finding compromises or alternative solutions that meet both parties' needs, rather than a simple yes or no answer. It's a collaborative effort to redefine the boundaries of your relationships to become healthier and more sustainable for all involved. This process often requires patience and understanding, and might involve some conflict, but the outcome can significantly improve the relationships.

If you find yourself consistently struggling to say no, even after practicing these techniques, consider seeking professional support. A therapist specializing in trauma and boundary setting can provide personalized guidance and support, helping you address the underlying issues that contribute to your difficulty in asserting your needs. They can provide a safe space to explore your past experiences, identify unhealthy patterns, and develop effective coping mechanisms for navigating challenging interpersonal dynamics. Therapy can be incredibly empowering in helping you reclaim your autonomy and build healthier relationships based on mutual respect.

Ultimately, saying no without guilt is a process of self-discovery and self-advocacy. It's about recognizing your own value and prioritizing your well-being. It's about building healthier relationships based on mutual respect and clear communication. It's a skill that requires practice, patience, and self-compassion, but it's a skill that yields significant rewards in terms of improved mental health, stronger relationships, and a greater sense of self-worth. The journey may involve discomfort and challenges, but the destination – a life lived with authentic self-expression and healthy boundaries – is well worth the effort.

Maintaining healthy boundaries is a multifaceted process that requires adapting our approach based on the unique dynamics of each relationship. While the core principles of clear communication and self-respect remain constant, the strategies for implementing them will vary depending on whether you're interacting with a romantic partner, family member, friend, or colleague. This section explores the nuances of boundary setting in different relationship contexts, providing practical examples and strategies to navigate these complexities.

Romantic Relationships: Romantic relationships, ideally, are built on mutual respect, trust, and open communication. However, even in healthy relationships, boundaries can become blurred. This often stems from a desire to please the partner, a fear of conflict, or unresolved past traumas that impact our sense of self-worth and autonomy. Setting boundaries in a romantic relationship requires a delicate balance between intimacy and individuality.

For instance, consider the issue of personal space. While physical affection is a vital component of many romantic relationships, it's essential to establish clear boundaries around what feels comfortable and acceptable. This might involve communicating preferences about physical touch, alone time, or the level of emotional intimacy desired. Avoid vague statements like, "I need some space," and instead be specific. "I enjoy spending time with you, but I need at least an hour to myself each evening to unwind and decompress before we engage in further activities." This provides clarity and prevents misunderstandings.

Financial boundaries are also crucial. Openly discussing financial goals, expectations, and individual contributions to shared expenses is essential for preventing resentment and conflict. Avoid assuming your partner shares the same financial values or comfort level with spending. Clear communication about financial decisions, joint accounts, and individual spending habits establishes a transparent and respectful financial relationship.

Emotional boundaries are particularly delicate. Sharing feelings and emotions is a vital part of a healthy romantic connection; however, it is crucial to establish limits on the level of emotional responsibility you carry for your partner. Avoid becoming solely responsible for their emotional well-being. It's acceptable to state, "I want to support you, but I'm not equipped to solve all your problems. Perhaps talking to a therapist or a trusted friend could help." This sets a healthy boundary while still demonstrating support.

Similarly, setting boundaries around time and activities is important. Maintaining individual interests and friendships outside of the romantic relationship safeguards personal identity and prevents feelings of suffocation or loss of self. If you need time for personal pursuits, communicate that clearly: "I value our time together, but I also need dedicated time each week to pursue my hobbies—yoga, running, or painting, for example. This is important for my well-being and also allows me to bring a refreshed perspective to our relationship."

Family Relationships: Family relationships often present unique challenges when it comes to boundary setting. Long-standing family dynamics, deeply ingrained patterns of behavior, and emotional complexities can make establishing and maintaining boundaries particularly difficult. Setting boundaries with family often requires more patience, empathy, and understanding, especially if you are dealing with family members who have difficulty respecting boundaries.

For example, setting boundaries around unsolicited advice or criticism is crucial. While family members may mean well, constant criticism or unsolicited advice can be draining and harmful. A response like, "I appreciate your concern, but I'm handling this situation in my own way," or "I'm open to your input, but right now I just need to process this on my own," gently but firmly establishes a boundary.

Boundaries around personal space and time with family also require careful consideration. Communicate clearly about your need for alone time or your limitations regarding visits or family gatherings. If you can only manage short visits due to work or other commitments, be direct and honest. "I'm so glad you're visiting. I only have a few hours available today to spend with you, but I look forward to catching up," avoids resentment and sets expectations appropriately.

Financial boundaries with family can also be a significant source of conflict. Establishing clear limits on lending money or providing financial support is essential to prevent exploitation or resentment. Avoid vague promises; be specific and direct about your capabilities and limits.

Emotional boundaries are particularly important in families, especially if you are dealing with emotionally demanding family members. Avoid becoming a dumping ground for their negative emotions. Learning to politely but firmly redirect conversations away from overwhelming or inappropriate emotional sharing is a key skill in maintaining healthy boundaries within family dynamics.

Friendships: Healthy friendships are characterized by mutual respect, support, and understanding. However, even in strong friendships, boundaries are necessary to maintain a balanced and sustainable relationship. Setting boundaries with friends often involves balancing needs and desires while ensuring that the friendship remains reciprocal and fulfilling.

Consider the issue of time commitment. Communicating your availability and setting limits on how much time you can dedicate to social activities is crucial to prevent your friendships from feeling overwhelming or one-sided. Instead of saying "I'm too busy," try "I'm really busy this week, but I'd love to catch up next week. How about Tuesday?"

Emotional boundaries are also important in friendships. While it's important to be supportive, it's also crucial to recognize that you cannot solve your friends' problems or be responsible for their emotional well-being. If a friend is consistently sharing overwhelming problems or negativity, you may need to set a boundary by saying, "I care about you and want to support you, but I'm not the right person to help you resolve this issue. Perhaps talking to a professional could be beneficial."

Boundaries related to shared activities and resources are essential. Clearly communicate your preferences and limits regarding borrowing items, sharing expenses, or participating in activities that you don't enjoy.

Work Relationships: Maintaining professional boundaries in the workplace is vital for both personal well-being and professional success. Setting clear boundaries can prevent burnout, enhance productivity, and foster more respectful interactions with colleagues and supervisors.

It's essential to establish boundaries around work hours and availability. Avoid consistently responding to work emails or messages outside of work hours unless absolutely necessary. Communicate clearly about your availability and expectations regarding after-hours work or requests. A firm but polite statement like, "I'm currently unavailable to respond to this request, however, I'll be happy to address it during business hours tomorrow" sets professional boundaries.

Setting boundaries with colleagues can involve addressing conflicts constructively, avoiding gossip, or politely declining requests that are outside your job description or capacity. Direct and honest communication is essential for establishing clear professional expectations. Avoid passive-aggressive behaviors; rather, address issues directly and respectfully, while staying professional.

Boundaries concerning workplace relationships are important to maintain professional conduct and avoid ethical concerns. Keeping interactions strictly professional, avoiding romantic entanglements that could compromise impartiality, and always respecting workplace policies safeguards against future issues.

Maintaining boundaries in any relationship is an ongoing process that requires regular review and adjustments. As relationships evolve, so too should the boundaries that define them. Regular check-ins with oneself and honest communication with others ensure that boundaries remain healthy and supportive of the relationship. Remember, setting boundaries is not about rejection or isolation; it's about self-respect, mutual understanding, and ultimately, building stronger, healthier, and more sustainable relationships.

Chapter 6: Building Resilience

Understanding resilience is crucial for navigating the complexities of life and building a fulfilling existence. Resilience isn't simply about avoiding hardship; it's about the capacity to adapt, overcome, and even thrive in the face of adversity. It's the ability to "bounce back" from setbacks, to learn from challenges, and to emerge stronger and more resourceful on the other side. This ability is not an innate trait bestowed upon a select few; rather, it's a skill that can be cultivated and strengthened over time through conscious effort and the development of effective coping strategies.

At its core, resilience is a dynamic process, not a static state. It's not about being impervious to pain or hardship; rather, it's about possessing the internal resources and external support networks to weather storms and emerge transformed. Think of a willow tree bending in a strong wind – it doesn't break because it's flexible, it adapts. Resilient individuals demonstrate a similar flexibility, adjusting their approaches and perspectives to navigate challenges effectively. They possess a deep understanding of their own strengths and weaknesses, and they actively cultivate strengths to counteract vulnerabilities.

Several key factors contribute significantly to an individual's overall resilience. One of the most important is a strong sense of self-efficacy – the belief in one's own ability to succeed in specific situations or accomplish a task. Individuals with high self-efficacy are more likely to approach challenges with confidence and determination, viewing them as opportunities for growth rather than insurmountable obstacles. They possess an internal locus of control, believing that their actions significantly influence outcomes, fostering proactive behavior in the face of adversity. Conversely, individuals with low self-efficacy may feel helpless and overwhelmed by challenges, hindering their ability to cope effectively.

Another critical component of resilience is optimism. Optimistic individuals tend to view setbacks as temporary and specific rather than permanent and pervasive. They maintain a hopeful outlook, focusing on potential solutions and positive outcomes even amidst difficult circumstances. This positive outlook provides a powerful buffer against stress and promotes proactive coping mechanisms. Studies have shown a strong correlation between optimism and resilience, demonstrating the vital role of positive thinking in navigating adversity. Conversely, pessimism can amplify negative emotions, making it harder to cope with challenges.

Social support also plays a pivotal role in fostering resilience. Strong social connections provide a sense of belonging, validation, and emotional support during difficult times. Resilient individuals often have a network of supportive friends, family members, and colleagues who offer practical assistance, emotional comfort, and encouragement. This social support acts as a buffer against stress, providing a sense of security and reducing feelings of isolation. Knowing you're not alone in facing challenges can significantly impact your ability to cope effectively. Conversely, a lack of social support can exacerbate the negative impact of stress and significantly hinder resilience.

Effective coping mechanisms are essential for building resilience. These are the strategies individuals employ to manage stress, regulate emotions, and navigate challenges. Some common coping mechanisms include problem-solving, seeking social support, engaging in self-care activities, and practicing mindfulness. Problem-solving involves actively identifying and addressing the root causes of difficulties, finding practical solutions, and implementing them effectively. Seeking social support entails reaching out to trusted individuals for emotional support, practical assistance, and advice. Self-care activities, such as exercise, healthy eating, sufficient sleep, and engaging in hobbies, are crucial for maintaining physical and mental well-being during stressful times. Mindfulness practices, such as meditation and deep breathing, promote emotional regulation and reduce stress.

The ability to regulate emotions is a cornerstone of resilience. Individuals who can effectively manage their emotional responses to challenging situations are better equipped to cope with adversity. This involves recognizing and accepting a wide range of emotions, developing strategies to manage intense feelings, and maintaining emotional balance in the face of stress. Techniques such as emotional regulation, cognitive reframing, and self-compassion can be invaluable in this process. Emotional regulation involves learning to identify and manage one's emotional responses, while cognitive reframing involves challenging negative thoughts and replacing them with more realistic and positive ones. Self-compassion involves treating oneself with kindness and understanding, especially during difficult times.

Meaning and purpose also significantly contribute to resilience. Individuals who find meaning and purpose in their lives are more likely to demonstrate greater resilience in the face of adversity. This sense of purpose provides motivation, hope, and a framework for navigating challenges. It helps to contextualize hardship within a broader perspective, fostering a sense of perseverance and strength. For example, someone who finds meaning in their work or their relationships may be more likely to persevere through difficult times, drawing strength from their values and beliefs.

The concept of "bouncing back" from adversity is a crucial aspect of resilience. It's not about avoiding setbacks entirely, but rather about having the capacity to recover from them and even grow from the experience. This involves learning from past mistakes, adapting to new challenges, and developing coping strategies that are effective and sustainable. Resilient individuals often use their past experiences to inform their future actions, using lessons learned to navigate future obstacles more effectively.

Examples of resilient individuals abound in various fields. Consider athletes who overcome injuries to return to their sport stronger than before. Their resilience stems from their dedication, their disciplined training, and their strong support systems. Entrepreneurs who experience business setbacks but persevere and build successful ventures also demonstrate remarkable resilience. Their determination, their adaptability, and their ability to learn from failures are all key factors in their success. Individuals who have survived traumatic experiences and rebuilt their lives also demonstrate incredible strength and resilience. Their ability to process their emotions, develop coping strategies, and rebuild their lives is a testament to the human capacity for resilience. They often demonstrate a capacity for self-compassion and a dedication to helping others, further strengthening their sense of purpose.

In conclusion, resilience is not a magical shield protecting us from life's challenges; it is a skill cultivated through conscious effort, self-awareness, and the development of effective coping strategies. By fostering a strong sense of self-efficacy, maintaining an optimistic outlook, building strong social support networks, developing effective coping mechanisms, and cultivating a sense of meaning and purpose, we can significantly enhance our resilience and navigate life's inevitable challenges with greater strength, grace, and adaptability. It's a journey of continuous growth, learning, and adaptation, a testament to the human capacity to overcome adversity and emerge stronger on the other side. The process is iterative, requiring ongoing self-reflection and adjustment as we face new challenges and develop new coping strategies. The ability to adapt and learn from setbacks is a crucial component of long-term resilience. Understanding the multifaceted nature of resilience empowers us to actively cultivate this valuable skill throughout our lives.

Developing effective coping mechanisms is paramount to building resilience. These aren't merely strategies for surviving difficult times; they're tools for thriving, for transforming challenges into opportunities for growth and self-discovery. The key lies in identifying strategies that resonate with your individual personality, values, and lifestyle. What works wonders for one person might be completely ineffective for another. This section will explore a diverse range of coping mechanisms, categorized for clarity, but remember that the most effective approach often involves a personalized combination of techniques.

Problem-Solving and Cognitive Restructuring: When faced with adversity, many individuals instinctively resort to problem-solving. This is a highly adaptive coping mechanism, involving a systematic approach to identifying the root causes of a problem, brainstorming potential solutions, evaluating their feasibility and potential consequences, and then implementing the chosen solution. However, effective problem-solving requires a clear and objective assessment of the situation, free from emotional biases. This is where cognitive restructuring comes into play.

Cognitive restructuring involves examining the thoughts and beliefs that underpin our emotional responses. Negative or distorted thoughts, such as catastrophizing (assuming the worst-case scenario) or overgeneralization (drawing broad conclusions from a single event), can significantly amplify stress and impair our ability to problem-solve effectively. Cognitive restructuring techniques help to challenge these unhelpful thought patterns, replacing them with more balanced and realistic perspectives. This process often involves identifying cognitive distortions, evaluating the evidence supporting and contradicting these distortions, and generating more adaptive thoughts. For instance, if someone experiences a setback at work and thinks, "I'm a complete failure," cognitive restructuring might involve challenging this thought by acknowledging past successes, considering external factors that contributed to the setback, and reframing the experience as a learning opportunity.

Journaling can be a powerful tool in both problem-solving and cognitive restructuring. By regularly writing down your thoughts and feelings, you can gain valuable insights into your emotional patterns and identify recurring negative thought patterns. This self-reflection can help you to challenge these patterns and develop more adaptive coping strategies. For example, journaling can help you track your progress in implementing solutions, note any obstacles encountered, and brainstorm alternative approaches. Furthermore, the act of writing itself can be therapeutic, providing an outlet for emotional expression and promoting self-awareness.

Emotional Regulation Techniques: Our emotional responses play a significant role in how we cope with stress. Effective emotional regulation involves developing the ability to identify, understand, and manage our emotional experiences without judgment. This doesn't mean suppressing or ignoring difficult emotions; rather, it involves developing healthy ways to process and express them. Several techniques can facilitate emotional regulation.

Mindfulness practices, such as meditation and deep breathing exercises, are powerful tools for enhancing emotional awareness and regulation. Mindfulness involves paying attention to the present moment without judgment, allowing you to observe your thoughts and feelings without getting swept away by them. Regular mindfulness practice can cultivate a sense of calm and emotional balance, enhancing your ability to respond to stressful situations with greater equanimity. Deep breathing exercises, in particular, can activate the parasympathetic nervous system, reducing the physiological effects of stress and promoting relaxation. Guided meditations, available through various apps and online resources, can provide structured support for developing mindfulness skills.

Somatic practices, such as yoga and tai chi, offer another avenue for emotional regulation. These practices integrate physical movement with mindfulness, promoting both physical and emotional well-being. By focusing on bodily sensations during movement, you can become more attuned to your emotional state and learn to manage physical tension related to stress. Yoga, for example, can help to release tension in the muscles, improving posture, and promoting relaxation. Tai chi, with its slow, deliberate movements and emphasis on breath, can help calm the nervous system and reduce anxiety.

Progressive muscle relaxation is another technique that directly targets physical tension related to stress. This involves systematically tensing and releasing different muscle groups, promoting relaxation throughout the body. It can be particularly helpful in managing physical symptoms of anxiety, such as muscle tension and headaches. Regular practice can enhance your ability to recognize and release tension, promoting a greater sense of overall well-being.

Seeking Social Support: Human beings are social creatures, and our connections with others play a crucial role in our well-being and resilience. Seeking social support doesn't just mean talking about your problems; it involves actively nurturing relationships with individuals who offer emotional support, practical assistance, and a sense of belonging. This might involve confiding in trusted friends or family members, joining support groups, or seeking professional help from a therapist or counselor.

Identifying your support system is a crucial first step. Think about the individuals in your life who offer consistent emotional support, who listen without judgment, and who offer practical help when needed. These individuals can act as buffers against stress, offering a sense of security and validation. Reaching out to these individuals, sharing your struggles, and accepting their support can significantly enhance your ability to cope with challenges.

If your existing support system is insufficient, consider actively building new connections. Joining support groups focused on specific challenges or interests can provide a sense of community and shared experience. These groups offer a safe space to share experiences, learn from others, and receive emotional support. Professional help from a therapist or counselor can also be invaluable, providing a structured framework for exploring your challenges, developing coping strategies, and processing emotions.

Self-Care Practices: Self-care is not a luxury; it's a necessity, particularly during times of stress. It encompasses a wide range of activities that nurture your physical, mental, and emotional well-being. This includes ensuring adequate sleep, maintaining a healthy diet, engaging in regular physical activity, and pursuing hobbies and activities that bring you joy.

Prioritizing sleep is crucial for both physical and mental health. Sufficient sleep allows your body and mind to rest and repair, strengthening your resilience to stress. Aim for 7-9 hours of quality sleep each night, and establish a consistent sleep schedule to regulate your body's natural sleep-wake cycle.

Maintaining a healthy diet provides your body with the nutrients it needs to function optimally. Focus on consuming whole, unprocessed foods, including fruits, vegetables, and lean proteins. Limit your intake of processed foods, sugary drinks, and excessive caffeine, which can negatively impact your mood and energy levels.

Regular physical activity releases endorphins, which have mood-boosting effects. Find activities you enjoy, whether it's walking, running, swimming, dancing, or team sports. Aim for at least 30 minutes of moderate-intensity exercise most days of the week.

Engaging in hobbies and activities that bring you joy is essential for maintaining a sense of balance and well-being. These activities can provide a distraction from stress, boost your mood, and promote a sense of accomplishment. Make time for these activities, even if it's just for a few minutes each day.

Worksheet: Identifying and Practicing Your Coping Mechanisms

This worksheet is designed to help you identify your preferred coping mechanisms and develop a personalized plan for managing stress and adversity.

1.

List five stressors you commonly face: (e.g., work deadlines, relationship conflicts, financial worries)

2.

For each stressor, list three coping mechanisms you've used in the past: (e.g., problem-solving, seeking social support, relaxation techniques)

3.

For each coping mechanism, rate its effectiveness on a scale of 1 to 5 (1 = not effective, 5 = very effective).

4.

Identify three new coping mechanisms you'd like to try: (e.g., mindfulness meditation, yoga, journaling)

5.

Create a personalized plan for implementing these coping mechanisms. This might involve scheduling specific times for practicing mindfulness, setting aside time for social connections, or incorporating self-care activities into your daily routine.

6.

Monitor your progress and adjust your plan as needed. Regularly assess the effectiveness of your coping mechanisms and make adjustments as necessary to ensure they continue to support your well-being.

By actively engaging in these coping strategies and utilizing the provided worksheet, you can build a strong foundation for resilience, empowering yourself to navigate life's inevitable challenges with greater strength, grace, and adaptability. Remember that building resilience is an ongoing process; it requires continuous self-reflection, learning, and adaptation. Embrace the journey, and celebrate your progress along the way.

Cultivating a strong sense of self-efficacy—the unshakeable belief in your capacity to succeed—is crucial for building resilience. It's the bedrock upon which you build your ability to navigate challenges, bounce back from setbacks, and ultimately, thrive. Without this inner confidence, even the most effective coping mechanisms can falter, leaving you vulnerable to feelings of helplessness and despair. This section will explore practical strategies to foster and strengthen your self-efficacy, empowering you to face adversity with conviction and a resilient spirit.

One of the most powerful ways to cultivate self-efficacy is through the deliberate setting and achievement of goals. This isn't about setting impossibly high aspirations destined for failure; rather, it's about strategically choosing goals that stretch your capabilities while remaining attainable. Start small, with manageable objectives that you can realistically accomplish. The feeling of accomplishment, no matter how small the task, is a potent catalyst for building self-belief.

For example, if you're struggling with procrastination, setting a goal of completing just one small task each day, such as responding to a single email or organizing a small area of your desk, can be a significant step forward. Each successful completion reinforces your belief in your ability to overcome procrastination, gradually building your confidence to tackle larger projects. Similarly, if you're working on improving your fitness, start with short walks, gradually increasing the duration and intensity as your fitness improves. The consistent progress will fuel your motivation and boost your sense of self-efficacy.

The key here is to break down larger goals into smaller, more manageable steps. This process, known as goal decomposition, allows you to focus on incremental progress, celebrating each milestone along the way. This approach prevents feelings of overwhelm and maintains your momentum, reinforcing your belief in your capabilities. For instance, if your goal is to write a book, break it down into smaller tasks: creating an outline, writing a chapter a week, editing each chapter, etc. Each completed step provides a sense of accomplishment, keeping you motivated and moving forward.

Beyond goal setting, actively seeking out challenges and pushing yourself beyond your comfort zone is vital for building self-efficacy. Stepping outside your comfort zone creates opportunities for learning and growth, revealing hidden strengths and capabilities you may not have known you possessed. The successful navigation of these challenges further strengthens your self-belief and reinforces your resilience.

Consider volunteering for a challenging project at work, learning a new skill, or participating in a public speaking event. These activities may feel daunting initially, but by successfully overcoming the initial fear and discomfort, you'll gain valuable experience and a significant boost to your self-efficacy. The sense of accomplishment derived from conquering a challenge outside your comfort zone is unparalleled and creates a positive feedback loop that encourages you to take on even greater challenges in the future.

Another crucial element in building self-efficacy is the power of positive self-talk. Our internal dialogue profoundly impacts our self-perception and our belief in our abilities. Negative self-talk, characterized by self-criticism, doubt, and pessimism, erodes self-efficacy, making it harder to persevere in the face of adversity. In contrast, positive self-talk, characterized by self-compassion, encouragement, and optimism, strengthens self-efficacy, boosting your motivation and resilience.

To cultivate positive self-talk, consciously replace negative thoughts with more balanced and supportive statements. For example, instead of thinking, "I'm going to fail this exam," try thinking, "I've studied hard, and I'm well-prepared. I can do this." Instead of saying, "I'm not good enough," try affirming, "I have strengths and capabilities, and I am continually growing and learning." This conscious effort to shift your inner dialogue from negativity to positivity is a powerful tool for strengthening your self-efficacy.

Observational learning, or learning by watching others succeed, also plays a significant role in building self-efficacy. By observing others overcome challenges similar to our own, we gain confidence in our ability to do the same. This is particularly effective when observing individuals who are similar to ourselves, as their successes feel more relatable and achievable.

For example, if you're struggling with public speaking, watching videos of successful public speakers who share similar backgrounds or experiences can boost your confidence in your own ability to deliver a compelling presentation. Similarly, if you're trying to manage a specific health condition, observing others effectively manage similar conditions can help to alleviate anxiety and reinforce your belief in your ability to manage your own condition effectively.

Furthermore, incorporating self-compassion into your approach to self-efficacy is paramount. Self-compassion involves treating yourself with the same kindness, understanding, and support that you would offer a close friend facing similar struggles. This means acknowledging your imperfections, accepting your vulnerability, and being kind to yourself during moments of difficulty. Self-compassion prevents self-criticism from undermining your self-efficacy and allows you to view setbacks as opportunities for growth and learning rather than indicators of personal failure.

Remember that building self-efficacy is an ongoing process, not a destination. It requires consistent effort, self-reflection, and a commitment to self-improvement. Setbacks are inevitable, but instead of viewing them as failures, embrace them as learning opportunities. Analyze what went wrong, adjust your approach, and keep moving forward. Celebrate your successes, no matter how small, and acknowledge your growth and progress along the way. By consistently employing the strategies outlined in this section, you'll cultivate a strong sense of self-efficacy, empowering you to navigate life's challenges with resilience, confidence, and a profound belief in your own capabilities. This belief is not merely a feeling; it's a powerful force that will propel you toward achieving your goals and living a fulfilling and resilient life. The journey of building self-efficacy is a deeply personal one; the strategies presented here serve as a framework, a guide to help you tailor your approach to your unique needs and experiences. Trust your own judgment, embrace the process, and celebrate every step you take towards cultivating a resilient and empowered self.

Learning from setbacks is not merely about bouncing back; it's about transforming challenges into catalysts for growth and resilience. It's about shifting our perspective from one of defeat to one of insightful analysis and strategic adaptation. Many individuals, particularly those who have experienced significant trauma, tend to dwell on setbacks, allowing negative self-talk and feelings of inadequacy to dominate their thinking. This can be a significant barrier to progress and can reinforce feelings of helplessness and hopelessness. However, by consciously reframing setbacks as opportunities for learning and growth, we can unlock valuable lessons that strengthen our resilience and enhance our ability to navigate future challenges with greater confidence and effectiveness.

The first step in learning from setbacks involves fostering a mindful awareness of our emotional responses. When faced with a setback, it's common to experience a range of difficult emotions: disappointment, frustration, anger, even shame or guilt. These emotions are natural and valid; they are part of the human experience. However, it's crucial to avoid becoming overwhelmed by these emotions. Instead, practice mindfulness by observing these emotions without judgment. Acknowledge their presence, allowing them to flow through you without getting carried away by them. This mindful awareness creates space for reflection and allows you to engage with the situation in a more rational and constructive manner. Techniques like deep breathing, progressive muscle relaxation, or mindful body scans can be particularly helpful in managing overwhelming emotions. These practices help to ground you in the present moment, reducing the intensity of emotional reactivity.

Once you've created emotional space, the next step is to conduct a thorough and objective analysis of the setback. Avoid placing blame or engaging in self-criticism. Instead, focus on identifying the contributing factors that led to the setback. Ask yourself questions such as: What were the specific challenges I faced? What resources or support did I have available? What strategies did I employ, and how effective were they? What external factors might have played a role? Consider external factors such as societal pressures, economic constraints, or unexpected life events that may have contributed to the setback. It is important to avoid overly simplistic explanations for setbacks, as these can prevent a comprehensive understanding. Consider utilizing a structured approach to analyzing your setbacks. For example, the "5 Whys" technique can help you to delve deeper into the root cause of the problem by repeatedly asking "Why?" until you reach the core issue. This approach often uncovers underlying patterns or weaknesses in your strategies or systems.

This analytical process should be conducted with a spirit of self-compassion. Remember that setbacks are a normal part of life; they are not indicators of personal failure. Treat yourself with the same kindness, understanding, and support that you would offer a close friend facing a similar challenge. Avoid harsh self-criticism; instead, focus on identifying areas for improvement and developing more effective strategies. Self-criticism is often counterproductive, undermining self-confidence and hindering the learning process.

The outcome of this analysis is not simply an identification of what went wrong; it's the generation of concrete actionable steps for improvement. This is where the transformative power of setbacks becomes truly apparent. Once you have identified the factors that contributed to the setback, you can begin to develop strategies to mitigate those factors in the future. This may involve acquiring new skills, seeking additional support, adjusting your approach, or developing more effective coping mechanisms. For example, if a setback stemmed from poor time management, you might consider adopting new time-management techniques such as the Pomodoro Technique or time blocking. If the setback was due to a lack of confidence, you might focus on building self-efficacy through goal setting, positive self-talk, and seeking out challenging opportunities. The process of developing and implementing these strategies is crucial for building resilience, reinforcing your self-belief, and enhancing your ability to navigate future challenges.

Furthermore, documenting your setbacks and lessons learned is an invaluable practice. Maintaining a journal or a digital log can provide a valuable record of your progress and allow you to track your growth over time. Each entry should document the setback, the analysis you conducted, and the strategies you developed to prevent similar setbacks in the future. This documentation provides a tangible record of your resilience-building journey and allows you to observe patterns and trends in your responses to challenges. It can also be a source of inspiration and encouragement during future difficulties, reminding you of your capacity for growth and adaptation. Regularly reviewing your journal entries can provide insights into recurring challenges and opportunities for personal growth. Identifying patterns in your responses to setbacks can help you to develop more targeted strategies for improving resilience.

Beyond personal reflection and analysis, seeking feedback from trusted sources can significantly enhance the learning process. This might involve discussing your setback with a mentor, a therapist, a close friend, or a family member. These individuals can provide valuable external perspectives, offering insights and suggestions that you may not have considered on your own. Choosing supportive individuals who will offer constructive feedback is crucial. Feedback should be specific and actionable, focusing on the specific aspects of the situation and offering suggestions for improvement. It's important to distinguish constructive criticism from unsolicited negative judgments. Remember that the purpose of seeking feedback is to learn from the experience, not to reinforce feelings of inadequacy or self-doubt.

Finally, remember that setbacks are not isolated events; they are interconnected parts of a larger narrative of growth and development. Embrace the journey of learning from setbacks as an integral part of your personal growth. This ongoing process of reflection, analysis, and adaptation is what truly builds resilience. It is a continuous cycle of learning and refinement, constantly shaping your abilities and expanding your capacity to navigate future challenges with greater ease and effectiveness. The ultimate goal is not to avoid setbacks entirely – that's unrealistic – but rather to develop the skills and mindset to effectively learn from them, transforming them from obstacles into stepping stones on your path to a more resilient and fulfilling life.

Building a strong support system is not a luxury, but a fundamental pillar of resilience. When life throws curveballs – be it a job loss, a relationship breakdown, a health scare, or the cumulative weight of everyday stressors – having a network of individuals you can rely on can significantly mitigate the impact and accelerate your recovery. This isn't about weakness; it's about recognizing the inherent strength in acknowledging our limitations and seeking help when needed. Humans are social creatures; our well-being is deeply intertwined with our connections to others. A robust support network provides a buffer against adversity, offering emotional, practical, and informational resources that can be invaluable during challenging periods.

The first step in building this network is honest self-reflection. Identify the individuals in your life who consistently offer you emotional support, practical assistance, or a listening ear. These might be family members, close friends, colleagues, mentors, or even members of your community. Consider the specific ways these people have supported you in the past. Did a friend offer a shoulder to cry on during a difficult time? Did a family member help with childcare while you dealt with a crisis? Did a colleague provide guidance and mentorship during a challenging project? By reflecting on past experiences, you can better understand the types of support you value most and identify the individuals who consistently provide that support. This process is crucial because it allows you to appreciate the existing support you already have and focus on strengthening those bonds.

Beyond identifying existing sources of support, consider expanding your network. This might involve reaching out to individuals you haven't connected with in a while or actively seeking out new relationships with people who share your interests or values. Joining a support group, volunteering in your community, or participating in activities that align with your passions are all excellent ways to broaden your social circle and create opportunities for meaningful connections. Remember, building a support network is an ongoing process; it's not something you do once and then forget about. Regularly nurturing these relationships is key to ensuring they remain strong and reliable during times of need.

The nature of support needed will also vary depending on the challenges you face. During a period of intense grief, you might need primarily emotional support, such as a listening ear and empathy. During a time of financial hardship, you might require practical support, such as assistance with childcare or help finding a new job. During a period of significant personal growth, you might seek informational support, such as guidance from a mentor or access to resources and training opportunities. Understanding your specific needs at any given moment allows you to identify the individuals best equipped to provide the support you require.

While relying on informal support networks (friends and family) is crucial, professional support often plays a vital role in building resilience. A therapist, counselor, or coach can provide a safe and confidential space to process difficult emotions, develop coping strategies, and work through challenging life experiences. They can offer objective perspectives and specialized techniques that may not be accessible through informal support systems. The choice of professional support should be tailored to your individual needs and preferences. Some individuals prefer cognitive behavioral therapy (CBT) to address negative thought patterns, while others find somatic experiencing or mindfulness-based practices more helpful for processing trauma or managing stress.

Selecting the right professional is critical. Do your research and find a therapist who specializes in the types of issues you're facing. Consider factors such as their experience, their therapeutic approach, and your comfort level with their personality and style. Many therapists offer free consultations, giving you the opportunity to discuss your needs and ensure a good fit. Don't hesitate to try out a few therapists until you find one who feels right for you. The therapeutic relationship itself is a significant part of the healing process, and finding the right therapist can be an invaluable step in building your resilience.

Seeking support doesn't imply weakness; it signifies self-awareness and a proactive approach to well-being. It's important to actively cultivate your support network, nurturing existing relationships and strategically expanding your connections. This involves clear communication; letting those around you know what you need and how they can best support you. This doesn't necessarily require a lengthy explanation or a dramatic outpouring of emotion; sometimes a simple, honest statement expressing vulnerability can be incredibly powerful. For instance, "I'm going through a tough time right now, and I could really use some extra support," or "I need some time to myself to process things," can go a long way in facilitating the support you need.

Conversely, be prepared to offer support to others. The reciprocal nature of support strengthens bonds and reinforces the sense of community and belonging so vital for resilience. Supporting others can also be a profound act of self-care, shifting focus away from personal struggles and fostering a sense of purpose and connection. This could involve listening actively without judgment, offering practical assistance, or simply being present for someone in need. The act of giving support can often be as beneficial to the giver as it is to the receiver.

Learning to accept support can be as challenging as offering it. Many individuals struggle with feelings of shame, guilt, or inadequacy when asking for help. This often stems from societal pressure to maintain a facade of strength and independence. However, embracing vulnerability is a courageous act, and recognizing the limitations of individual strength is a sign of maturity and self-awareness. Allow yourself to accept support without judgment or self-criticism. Recognize that asking for help is not a sign of weakness but rather a testament to your commitment to your well-being and a practical strategy for navigating difficult times.

This acceptance also necessitates understanding the limitations of your support system. Friends and family, while well-meaning, might not always possess the expertise or emotional capacity to provide the level of support required. This isn't a reflection on their character; it's simply acknowledging the different roles various individuals play in our lives. Sometimes, seeking professional support alongside your informal networks is necessary for optimal well-being. Recognizing these boundaries is crucial for avoiding disillusionment and frustration.

Furthermore, the support network should be diverse and multi-faceted. Relying solely on one person or a small group can create an unhealthy dependence and increase vulnerability if that support source is unavailable or compromised. A diversified network offers resilience against potential disruptions and strengthens your overall capacity to weather various storms. This might mean having close friends, family members, professional contacts, community members, and potentially a therapist, creating a robust system of support across multiple domains of your life.

Finally, building resilience isn't a solitary pursuit; it's a collaborative effort. It's about fostering healthy relationships, actively participating in your support network, and cultivating a culture of mutual support and understanding. By embracing vulnerability, fostering meaningful connections, and utilizing both informal and professional support, you can build a resilient foundation that empowers you to navigate life's inevitable challenges with greater strength and grace. This process of building and nurturing a robust support network isn't merely about surviving; it's about thriving, even in the face of adversity.

Chapter 7: Seeking Support and Resources

Recognizing the need for professional support isn't always straightforward. It's often a gradual realization, a subtle shift in how you feel and function, rather than a sudden, dramatic event. Many individuals hesitate to seek professional help, fueled by misconceptions about therapy, societal stigma, or personal anxieties. However, understanding the signs and addressing these hesitations is crucial for accessing the support you deserve.

One of the most common indicators is persistent feelings of sadness, hopelessness, or overwhelming anxiety that don't subside within a reasonable timeframe. While everyone experiences periods of sadness or stress, the key difference lies in the duration and intensity of these emotions. If you're feeling consistently low, experiencing significant interference with your daily life, and struggling to find relief through self-care techniques, it's a strong signal to consider professional assistance. This isn't about weakness; it's about recognizing that your emotional well-being is just as important as your physical health. Prolonged sadness or anxiety can manifest in various ways, impacting your sleep, appetite, concentration, energy levels, and relationships. For example, consistently neglecting your personal hygiene, isolating yourself from loved ones, or struggling to maintain basic daily routines like showering or eating can be significant warning signs.

Another sign that professional help might be beneficial is experiencing persistent difficulty managing stress. Stress is an inherent part of life, but if you find yourself constantly overwhelmed, unable to cope with everyday challenges, or resorting to unhealthy coping mechanisms like excessive substance use or self-harm, seeking professional support is essential. Healthy stress management involves employing various coping strategies, such as exercise, mindfulness, spending time in nature, or engaging in hobbies. However, if these strategies are proving ineffective, or if you find yourself relying on unhealthy coping mechanisms, a therapist can guide you in developing more effective and sustainable strategies. Furthermore, chronic stress can manifest physically, leading to headaches, digestive issues, muscle tension, or sleep disturbances. If your physical health is suffering as a result of ongoing stress, it's crucial to seek professional intervention. For instance, if you find yourself experiencing chronic headaches, digestive problems, or sleep disturbances despite trying various self-care methods, it is advisable to speak with both a physician and a therapist to address the underlying emotional and physical stressors.

Traumatic experiences, whether recent or from the past, can profoundly impact mental health. Trauma can manifest in various ways, including flashbacks, nightmares, intrusive thoughts, avoidance behaviors, emotional numbness, or difficulty regulating emotions. If you are struggling to process a traumatic experience and are experiencing significant emotional distress, professional help is highly recommended. A therapist can provide a safe and supportive environment to process these experiences and develop healthy coping mechanisms, helping you regain a sense of control and safety. Trauma therapy often involves specialized techniques like EMDR (Eye Movement Desensitization and Reprocessing) or somatic experiencing, which are designed to address the physical and emotional aspects of trauma.

Relationship difficulties, particularly those characterized by conflict, abuse, or betrayal, can severely impact mental well-being. If your relationships are consistently causing significant distress, impacting your self-esteem, or hindering your personal growth, seeking professional help can offer valuable guidance. A therapist can assist in exploring unhealthy relationship patterns, developing communication skills, and establishing healthier boundaries. For example, if you are experiencing patterns of domestic violence or emotional abuse, seeking professional help is crucial, not only for your mental health but also for your safety. Relationship therapy can also be beneficial for couples or families facing significant challenges.

Substance use disorders, whether involving alcohol, drugs, or other substances, are serious conditions that require professional intervention. If you're struggling to control your substance use, experiencing negative consequences as a result, or finding it difficult to stop despite wanting to, seeking help is essential. Therapists specializing in addiction treatment can provide evidence-based therapies, support groups, and resources to help you navigate the recovery process. It's important to remember that addiction is a treatable condition, and seeking professional help is a sign of strength and commitment to recovery.

Changes in sleep patterns, appetite, or energy levels can also be indicative of underlying mental health issues. While occasional fluctuations are normal, persistent changes that significantly disrupt your daily life warrant professional attention. For instance, if you are experiencing chronic insomnia, significant weight loss or gain, or consistently low energy levels despite getting adequate rest, it's crucial to consult with a healthcare professional. These symptoms could indicate a range of conditions, including depression, anxiety, or other mental health disorders. A thorough medical evaluation is necessary to rule out any physical causes before addressing the emotional aspects.

Suicidal thoughts or self-harm behaviors are critical warning signs that require immediate professional intervention. If you are having thoughts of harming yourself or others, please reach out for help immediately.

There are many resources available to provide support and guidance, including crisis hotlines, emergency services, and mental health professionals. Remember, you are not alone, and help is available. Do not hesitate to contact a crisis hotline, emergency room, or a trusted mental health professional.

Beyond specific symptoms, there are other important factors to consider. If your daily functioning is severely impaired, if you are struggling to maintain your responsibilities at work, school, or home, or if your relationships are significantly strained, these are all signs that seeking professional help may be beneficial. This could involve experiencing difficulty concentrating, decreased productivity, social withdrawal, or increased conflict with family or friends. These are all subtle indicators that your overall well-being is compromised and may benefit from professional intervention.

Hesitations about seeking help are common, but understanding these hesitations can help overcome them. Many people worry about the stigma associated with mental health treatment. Society has historically stigmatized mental illness, but attitudes are changing, and seeking professional help is becoming increasingly common and accepted. Remember that seeking help is a sign of strength, not weakness. It demonstrates self-awareness and a commitment to your well-being.

Financial concerns often deter individuals from seeking professional help. However, many therapists offer sliding scale fees, and resources like insurance coverage and community mental health centers can make treatment more affordable. Exploring options and inquiring about financial assistance can alleviate these concerns and make professional support accessible.

Fear of judgment from others is another common hesitation. Sharing your struggles with a therapist creates a confidential and safe space for vulnerability. Therapists are trained professionals bound by confidentiality and are committed to providing non-judgmental support. Choosing a therapist who you feel comfortable with is crucial in building a strong therapeutic relationship.

Uncertainty about the process of finding a therapist can also be daunting. However, resources like online directories and referrals from primary care physicians can help you find a therapist who meets your needs and preferences. Many therapists offer initial consultations, allowing you to discuss your concerns and determine if it's a good fit before committing to ongoing treatment.

Ultimately, the decision to seek professional help is a personal one. There is no shame in acknowledging your limitations and seeking support when needed. Recognizing the signs, addressing your hesitations, and proactively seeking help are vital steps toward improving your well-being and building a more resilient future. Your mental health is just as important as your physical health, and seeking professional assistance is an act of self-care and commitment to your overall well-being. Remember, it takes courage to seek help, and that courage is a testament to your strength and commitment to a healthier, happier life.

Finding the right therapist or counselor is a crucial step in your journey toward healing and well-being. It's not simply about finding someone who's licensed; it's about finding a professional who understands your specific needs, resonates with your personality, and employs therapeutic approaches that align with your preferences and goals. This process may require some exploration and self-reflection, but the investment is worthwhile. The therapeutic relationship is a partnership, and selecting a compatible therapist is foundational to its success.

One of the first considerations is the therapist's specialization. Not all therapists are created equal; many specialize in specific areas of mental health. If you've experienced trauma, for instance, you'll want to find a therapist experienced in trauma-informed care. This might involve seeking someone trained in EMDR (Eye Movement Desensitization and Reprocessing), somatic experiencing, or other evidence-based trauma treatment modalities. Similarly, if you're struggling with addiction, seeking a therapist specializing in substance abuse disorders is essential. They possess specialized knowledge and skills in addressing the complexities of addiction, including relapse prevention and coping mechanisms. If you're dealing with relationship issues, a therapist with expertise in couples or family therapy might be the best fit. Likewise, if your struggles involve anxiety or depression, finding a therapist experienced in cognitive behavioral therapy (CBT), dialectical behavior therapy (DBT), or other relevant approaches can be beneficial. Don't hesitate to inquire about a therapist's specific training and experience; it's a vital part of finding the right match. Many therapists' websites provide detailed information on their areas of expertise.

Beyond specialization, the therapist's treatment modality is another key factor. Treatment modalities refer to the specific techniques and approaches a therapist uses in therapy. CBT, for example, focuses on identifying and changing negative thought patterns and behaviors. DBT emphasizes emotional regulation and distress tolerance skills.

Psychodynamic therapy explores unconscious patterns and past experiences to understand present-day difficulties. Mindfulness-based therapies incorporate meditation and other mindfulness practices to cultivate self-awareness and emotional regulation. Somatic therapies address the mind-body connection, recognizing that trauma and other emotional issues are often stored in the body. Understanding your preferences and exploring various modalities can help you find a therapist whose approach aligns with your needs and comfort level. Researching different therapeutic approaches can provide valuable insight and help you communicate your preferences during your initial consultation.

The therapeutic relationship itself is paramount. You should feel comfortable, safe, and respected in the therapeutic space. A good therapist will create an environment of trust and empathy, offering unconditional positive regard. You should feel heard and understood, without judgment or criticism. The therapist should be able to create a therapeutic alliance—a collaborative partnership—where you feel empowered and actively involved in your treatment. If you feel uncomfortable, unheard, or dismissed, it's perfectly acceptable to seek a different therapist. The therapeutic relationship is a cornerstone of successful therapy, and finding a therapist with whom you connect is crucial. Trust your intuition; if something doesn't feel right, it likely isn't.

Insurance coverage is a practical consideration that shouldn't be overlooked. Before committing to a therapist, inquire about their insurance policies and whether they accept your plan. Many therapists offer sliding scale fees, accommodating clients' financial limitations. If insurance coverage isn't sufficient, consider exploring community mental health centers, which often provide affordable or subsidized services. Financial constraints shouldn't prevent you from accessing necessary support; resources are available to make mental healthcare more accessible. Don't hesitate to be upfront about your financial limitations; many therapists are understanding and willing to work with you.

Utilizing resources to find a suitable therapist is critical. Many online directories provide extensive listings of therapists, often with detailed profiles indicating their specializations, treatment modalities, and insurance affiliations. Psychology Today, GoodTherapy, and Zocdoc are examples of such platforms. You can filter your search based on various criteria, including location, specialization, insurance acceptance, and even gender or cultural background. These online directories offer a convenient and comprehensive way to begin your search. Furthermore, your primary care physician or psychiatrist can often provide referrals to therapists in your area. These referrals can offer valuable insights and guidance, particularly if you are uncertain where to begin your search. Seeking advice from a trusted friend, family member, or support group might also lead you to helpful suggestions or testimonials.

Once you've identified potential therapists, scheduling initial consultations is highly recommended. This allows you to meet with the therapist, discuss your needs and goals, and determine if it's a good fit. Many therapists offer free or low-cost consultations to assess compatibility. During this consultation, you should feel free to ask any questions about the therapist's approach, experience, and therapeutic style. You can also express your preferences and concerns, ensuring your needs are clearly understood. This is your opportunity to gauge the therapeutic connection and ensure you feel comfortable and confident in choosing this therapist as your partner in healing. It's perfectly acceptable to meet with several therapists before deciding which one is the best fit.

The process of finding the right therapist may involve some trial and error. It's a personal journey, and finding the ideal therapist is not a one-size-fits-all experience. Don't feel pressured to settle for the first therapist you find; continue your search until you feel confident in the therapeutic alliance. Your comfort and trust in your therapist are foundational to the success of your therapy journey. Remember, you're investing in your well-being, and finding the right therapist is a crucial investment in your future health and happiness. The time and effort expended in finding the right professional is far outweighed by the benefits of receiving effective and personalized support. This commitment to finding the ideal therapeutic partner demonstrates your dedication to your own well-being and is a significant step towards creating lasting positive change in your life. Remember, you deserve to feel supported and understood in your journey towards healing.

The journey towards healing from trauma and stress often involves exploring different therapeutic approaches. Understanding the various types of therapy available empowers you to make informed decisions about your treatment, fostering a more active and collaborative partnership with your therapist. This section provides a comprehensive overview of several common and effective therapy modalities, emphasizing their unique strengths and applications.

Cognitive Behavioral Therapy (CBT) stands as a prominent evidence-based approach, widely recognized for its efficacy in treating a broad range of mental health conditions, including anxiety, depression, and PTSD. CBT operates on the principle that our thoughts, feelings, and behaviors are interconnected. Negative or unhelpful thought patterns, often rooted in cognitive distortions, can fuel negative emotions and lead to maladaptive behaviors. CBT aims to identify and challenge these distorted thought patterns, replacing them with more realistic and balanced perspectives. Through this process, individuals learn to manage their emotions more effectively and develop healthier coping mechanisms. A core component of CBT involves behavioral experiments, where clients test out new ways of thinking and behaving in real-life situations, reinforcing positive changes. For instance, a person struggling with social anxiety might use CBT to gradually expose themselves to social situations, challenging their negative beliefs about social interactions. This gradual exposure, combined with cognitive restructuring, helps them build confidence and reduce their anxiety levels over time. The structured nature of CBT, with its emphasis on goal setting and progress tracking, provides a sense of control and empowers individuals to actively participate in their recovery.

Trauma-focused therapies are specifically designed to address the impact of traumatic experiences on individuals. These therapies recognize the unique challenges posed by trauma, acknowledging its pervasive influence on emotions, thoughts, and physical sensations. Eye Movement Desensitization and Reprocessing (EMDR) is a widely used trauma-focused therapy that employs bilateral stimulation—such as eye movements, tapping, or sounds—to help individuals process traumatic memories. The premise is that bilateral stimulation facilitates the processing of traumatic memories, reducing their emotional intensity and allowing for integration into the individual's overall experience. EMDR is often used in conjunction with other therapeutic approaches, such as CBT, to help individuals develop coping skills and address any lingering emotional or behavioral difficulties. Another prominent trauma-focused therapy is somatic experiencing (SE). Unlike traditional talk therapy, SE focuses on the body's sensations and responses to trauma. It recognizes that trauma is often stored in the body, manifesting as physical symptoms such as muscle tension, pain, or digestive issues. Through gentle body awareness exercises and mindful movement, SE helps individuals release trapped trauma and regain a sense of safety and control over their bodies. Prolonged Exposure (PE) is another evidence-based therapy for trauma, which involves gradual and repeated exposure to trauma-related memories, feelings, and situations. This method helps individuals confront their trauma in a safe and controlled environment, diminishing its power and intensity over time. The choice of trauma-focused therapy will depend upon the individual's specific needs and preferences, and often involves consultation with a therapist specializing in trauma treatment.

Mindfulness-based therapies leverage mindfulness practices, such as meditation and body scan meditation, to cultivate self-awareness and enhance emotional regulation. These therapies emphasize the present moment, encouraging individuals to observe their thoughts and feelings without judgment. By fostering greater self-awareness, individuals can develop a more compassionate relationship with themselves and their experiences. Mindfulness-Based Stress Reduction (MBSR) is a well-established program that incorporates mindfulness meditation, body scan, gentle yoga, and mindful movement to reduce stress and improve overall well-being. It teaches individuals techniques to manage stress, anxiety, and chronic pain. Mindfulness-Based Cognitive Therapy (MBCT) combines mindfulness practices with cognitive therapy techniques, targeting individuals who experience recurrent depressive episodes. By developing greater awareness of their thoughts and feelings, participants learn to identify and interrupt negative thought patterns, reducing their vulnerability to depression. Acceptance and Commitment Therapy (ACT) is another mindfulness-based approach that emphasizes acceptance of difficult thoughts and feelings, fostering commitment to values-based actions. ACT helps individuals develop psychological flexibility, enabling them to respond to challenges more effectively without being controlled by their thoughts and emotions. These mindfulness-based techniques can be integrated into various other therapeutic modalities, strengthening their overall effectiveness.

Psychodynamic therapy, with its roots in the work of Sigmund Freud, emphasizes exploring unconscious patterns and past experiences to understand present-day difficulties. It posits that unresolved conflicts and past traumas can significantly impact current relationships, emotions, and behaviors. Through the therapeutic relationship, individuals gain insight into their unconscious processes, revealing underlying patterns that contribute to their struggles. This often involves exploring early childhood experiences, attachment patterns, and recurring relational dynamics. Through interpretation and exploration, individuals can achieve greater self-understanding and work towards healthier patterns of relating to themselves and others. While less focused on symptom reduction in the short-term, compared to CBT, psychodynamic therapy aims for deeper, more enduring change by addressing the root causes of emotional distress. This approach can be particularly helpful for individuals grappling with complex or long-standing emotional issues.

Dialectical Behavior Therapy (DBT) is a highly effective therapy for individuals struggling with intense emotions and self-destructive behaviors, particularly those with borderline personality disorder (BPD). DBT integrates mindfulness techniques with behavioral strategies, emphasizing emotional regulation, distress tolerance, interpersonal effectiveness, and mindfulness skills. The dialectical aspect of DBT acknowledges the tension between acceptance and change, encouraging individuals to accept their current experiences while actively working towards positive change. DBT skills training groups are often a core component of DBT therapy, providing individuals with structured learning opportunities to build coping skills. These skills are then practiced and reinforced during individual therapy sessions, where clients can explore their challenges and apply their newly acquired skills in real-life situations.

Family therapy focuses on the dynamics within a family system, addressing relational patterns and communication styles that contribute to emotional distress. Family therapy assumes that individuals' problems are often intertwined with family relationships. The therapist works with the entire family unit to identify dysfunctional patterns and improve communication and interactions. This approach can be particularly effective for families struggling with conflict, substance abuse, or other challenges that impact multiple family members. Similarly, couples therapy aims to improve communication and conflict resolution skills between partners, promoting a healthier and more fulfilling relationship. Couples therapy often employs various techniques, including communication exercises, conflict resolution strategies, and exploring individual needs and perspectives.

Group therapy offers a supportive environment where individuals can share their experiences, learn from others, and develop a sense of community. Group therapy can be particularly beneficial for individuals who feel isolated or struggle with social connection. The shared experience of group members fosters a sense of validation and hope, reducing feelings of loneliness and shame. The dynamics within a group provide opportunities for learning about interpersonal relationships, practicing social skills, and receiving feedback from peers. The composition of the group – homogeneous (e.g., all experiencing PTSD) or heterogeneous (a mix of issues) – will be determined based on therapeutic goals.

The selection of a specific therapy modality is a highly individualized process, dependent upon several factors including the nature of the challenges faced, personal preferences, and the therapist's expertise. It's essential to have open communication with your therapist, discussing your goals and preferences to ensure that the chosen approach aligns with your needs. Many therapists employ an integrative approach, drawing upon various modalities to create a personalized treatment plan tailored to the individual's unique circumstances. Moreover, the therapeutic relationship itself is a crucial element, emphasizing the importance of feeling safe, understood, and supported within the therapeutic context. It is not uncommon to try different approaches before finding the best fit. Remember, the goal is to find a collaborative partnership with a therapist who provides the tools and support needed to navigate your journey towards healing and well-being. The investment in this process is an investment in your future health and happiness.

The therapeutic journey is rarely a solitary one. While individual therapy provides crucial one-on-one support and personalized treatment, the power of connection and shared experience cannot be underestimated. This is where support groups and peer support networks become invaluable assets in the recovery process from trauma and stress. These settings offer a unique opportunity to connect with others who understand the complexities and challenges of navigating similar experiences. The shared understanding within these groups creates a safe and validating space where individuals can feel less alone in their struggles, fostering a sense of belonging and reducing the pervasive sense of isolation that often accompanies trauma.

The benefits of support groups extend beyond simply sharing experiences. The act of expressing one's trauma in a supportive environment can be deeply cathartic, helping individuals process emotions and gain valuable perspective. Hearing from others who have successfully navigated similar challenges offers hope and inspiration, demonstrating that recovery is possible. Support groups also provide a platform for learning coping mechanisms and strategies from peers, enriching the toolbox of techniques already learned in individual therapy. This peer-to-peer exchange of practical tips and emotional support can significantly enhance the effectiveness of professional treatment.

The structure and focus of support groups vary widely. Some are specifically designed for individuals with particular types of trauma, such as PTSD following military service, sexual assault, or childhood abuse. These specialized groups offer a tailored environment where participants share a common language and understanding of the unique challenges associated with their specific trauma. Other groups might encompass a broader range of experiences, offering a more diverse and inclusive setting. This inclusivity can be valuable for those whose experiences might not neatly fall into one specific category or those seeking a wider perspective on trauma recovery.

Regardless of their focus, effective support groups typically prioritize safety, confidentiality, and mutual respect. Ground rules are usually established to ensure a supportive and non-judgmental atmosphere. These rules often involve respecting others' experiences, refraining from offering unsolicited advice or judgment, and maintaining confidentiality within the group. A skilled facilitator, trained in trauma-informed care, often guides the group discussions. Their role is not to provide therapy, but rather to manage the group dynamics, ensuring everyone feels heard and respected while promoting productive communication and constructive interactions. Their expertise helps navigate potentially sensitive or challenging conversations, ensuring that the group remains a supportive and safe environment for all participants.

For individuals who might find the structured setting of a formal support group challenging, or who prefer a more informal approach, peer support networks offer a less structured alternative. These networks might involve online forums, social media groups, or even informal gatherings of individuals with shared experiences. While lacking the formal structure and guidance of a therapist-led group, peer support networks still provide valuable opportunities for connection, shared experience, and mutual support. The informal nature can be beneficial for individuals who prefer a less formal setting or who feel more comfortable connecting with others in a less structured environment.

However, it's crucial to approach online peer support networks with caution. While many offer valuable support and connections, the anonymity of the internet can also lead to misinformation, unhelpful advice, or potentially triggering content. Therefore, careful selection of online resources, including verification of the group's moderation practices and established guidelines for respectful interaction, is important. Prioritizing groups with clear guidelines and active moderation is essential to ensuring a positive and supportive experience.

Finding a suitable support group or peer support network involves some research and exploration. Many local mental health organizations, hospitals, and community centers offer support groups for individuals recovering from trauma. Websites such as the Substance Abuse and Mental Health Services Administration (SAMHSA) and the National Alliance on Mental Illness (NAMI) provide valuable resources to locate local support groups and peer support programs. Online search engines can also be helpful, but should be used cautiously, as mentioned previously. It's advisable to contact the organization or group directly to learn more about their specific focus, approach, and overall environment before committing to participation.

Beyond formally structured support groups and online networks, building supportive relationships with trusted friends, family members, and other individuals in one's life is crucial. While these relationships may not replicate the specific benefits of a structured support group, their importance in promoting well-being and facilitating recovery should not be underestimated. Open communication with loved ones about one's experiences and challenges can reduce feelings of isolation and enhance emotional support. It is vital, however, that individuals choose supportive relationships carefully. Those close to them must be capable and willing to listen without judgment, providing a supportive environment for processing difficult emotions and memories.

The decision to participate in a support group is a personal one, and it's entirely acceptable to try out different groups or approaches before finding the right fit. Some individuals may find that structured support groups provide the ideal level of support and guidance, while others may prefer the informal nature of peer support networks or the comfort of their pre-existing support systems. There is no single right answer; the key is to find a method of support that feels comfortable, safe, and conducive to healing.

The integration of support groups and peer support into a holistic treatment plan can significantly amplify the benefits of individual therapy and other therapeutic interventions. These approaches often complement professional treatment by offering a sense of community, validation, and shared understanding, accelerating the healing process. By combining the personalized attention of individual therapy with the collective strength and shared experience of a supportive community, individuals can embark on a more comprehensive and effective path towards recovery from trauma and stress. Remember, reaching out for support is a sign of strength, not weakness. It is a courageous step towards healing and rebuilding a life filled with resilience and well-being. The path to recovery is often multifaceted and uniquely personal, and the incorporation of these supplemental support systems can prove invaluable in achieving lasting healing and growth. The ongoing support provided by peers and professionals alike serves as a vital cornerstone in the journey towards lasting mental health and well-being.

The journey through trauma is a complex and deeply personal one. While professional therapeutic interventions form a critical foundation for recovery, recognizing the significant role that social support plays in this process is vital. Support groups and peer support networks offer a space where individuals can connect with others who understand the subtleties and intricacies of navigating similar experiences. The shared understanding within these groups cultivates a sense of belonging and reduces the isolating feelings often associated with trauma. Through sharing experiences, learning from others, and developing coping strategies, individuals can gain invaluable perspective and build resilience. Furthermore, the emotional support received within these settings can significantly bolster the efficacy of individual therapy, accelerating the healing process and fostering a stronger sense of self.

The importance of finding a supportive network extends beyond formal support groups. Building strong relationships with trusted friends, family, and colleagues also contributes significantly to recovery. The presence of supportive individuals who listen without judgment, offering empathy and understanding, can alleviate feelings of isolation and provide much-needed emotional sustenance. Choosing such relationships carefully is crucial. Support should be offered in a manner that respects personal boundaries and does not impose undue pressure or expectations. It is essential to cultivate a support system that prioritizes empathy, understanding, and respect.

It is vital to emphasize that while peer support and support groups can be exceptionally beneficial tools in recovery, they are not replacements for professional therapeutic interventions. Formal therapy with a licensed professional often provides the specialized knowledge, skills, and expertise needed to address the complex psychological impact of trauma. Support groups and peer support networks work best when used as a complement to professional therapy, enhancing the overall effectiveness of the healing process. A holistic approach, integrating various forms of support and professional guidance, offers the most comprehensive path toward recovery.

The search for suitable support groups and peer support networks requires thoughtful consideration. When seeking these resources, consider the type of trauma experienced, personal preferences for group dynamics, and the availability of resources within one's community. Several organizations and online platforms offer directories of support groups and peer support networks. These resources can help individuals find groups that align with their specific needs and preferences. Always verify the credibility and safety of any group or network before committing to participation. It is crucial to prioritize groups that adhere to clear guidelines, uphold confidentiality, and maintain a supportive and non-judgmental environment.

In conclusion, embracing the power of support groups and peer support is a crucial step in the path to recovery from trauma. These resources offer a sense of community, shared understanding, and validation that can significantly enhance the effectiveness of professional treatment. By combining the benefits of individual therapy with the collective strength of a supportive community, individuals can navigate the complexities of trauma and emerge with greater resilience, hope, and well-being. Remember, reaching out for support is a sign of strength and a crucial element in the journey towards lasting healing and growth. The investment in building a supportive network is an investment in your mental and emotional health, laying the groundwork for a more fulfilling and resilient future.

The previous sections emphasized the crucial role of interpersonal support in trauma recovery, highlighting the benefits of support groups and peer networks. However, the digital age offers a wealth of additional resources that can significantly complement these in-person interactions. This section explores the diverse landscape of online tools and self-help resources available to aid in the healing process, emphasizing the importance of critical evaluation and mindful selection.

The internet provides a vast array of applications, websites, and platforms specifically designed to support mental well-being and trauma recovery. Many apps focus on mindfulness practices, offering guided meditations, breathing exercises, and body scans. These tools can be particularly helpful in managing symptoms of anxiety, stress, and PTSD. Mindfulness apps often incorporate elements of cognitive behavioral therapy (CBT) and dialectical behavior therapy (DBT), integrating practical techniques for managing challenging thoughts and emotions. Examples include Calm, Headspace, and Insight Timer, each offering a range of guided meditations tailored to different needs and preferences. Some apps even incorporate personalized programs adapted to individual progress and goals. These programs can provide a structured approach to mindfulness practice, helping users build consistent habits and track their progress over time. The accessibility of these apps, available anytime and anywhere on smartphones and tablets, offers significant advantages for individuals who might find it challenging to attend regular in-person therapy sessions or support group meetings. The convenience allows for integration into daily routines, making mindfulness practice a more readily accessible part of life.

Beyond mindfulness apps, numerous online platforms offer self-help resources for managing stress and trauma. Many websites provide information on trauma-informed therapies, coping strategies, and self-care techniques. These platforms often include articles, videos, and downloadable workbooks that offer practical guidance and support. It's crucial, however, to exercise caution when accessing online information. Not all resources are created equal, and some may contain inaccurate, misleading, or even harmful information. Therefore, it's essential to carefully vet the credibility of any online source before utilizing its content. Look for sites affiliated with reputable organizations such as the National Institute of Mental Health (NIMH), the American Psychological Association (APA), or the Substance Abuse and Mental Health Services Administration (SAMHSA). These organizations typically adhere to strict guidelines ensuring the accuracy and ethical nature of the information they provide. Cross-referencing information from multiple reputable sources can help verify its accuracy and provide a more comprehensive understanding of the topic.

While online resources offer valuable support, it's crucial to remember that they should not replace professional therapeutic interventions. Self-help tools are most effective when used as a supplement to professional guidance, not as a sole form of treatment. They can help individuals manage symptoms, practice coping mechanisms, and build resilience, but they cannot address the underlying complexities of trauma in the same way that a trained therapist can. A professional therapist can provide personalized guidance, address specific triggers, and help individuals process traumatic experiences safely and effectively.

The therapist can also work to ensure that the self-help tools being used are appropriate and safe for the individual's specific circumstances. The combination of professional guidance and self-directed learning can foster a more comprehensive and effective approach to recovery. The therapist can also assist the individual in identifying and avoiding unreliable or harmful online content.

Furthermore, the use of online resources necessitates a critical and discerning approach. The anonymity of the internet can lead to misinformation, inaccurate advice, or even potentially triggering content. It's imperative to prioritize platforms and resources that adhere to established ethical guidelines and emphasize factual information. Look for sites that clearly state their credentials and affiliations, and that offer evidence-based information rather than unsubstantiated claims. Be cautious of websites or forums promoting unproven treatments or making unsubstantiated promises of rapid healing. A healthy skepticism, coupled with a thorough evaluation of the source's credibility, is essential in navigating the vast landscape of online resources. Remember that your mental health and well-being are paramount, and it's crucial to protect yourself from potentially harmful information.

Many online forums and communities dedicated to trauma recovery can also be beneficial. These platforms offer opportunities to connect with others who understand the complexities of navigating similar experiences. Sharing experiences within a supportive online environment can help individuals feel less alone and reduce feelings of isolation. However, it is crucial to approach online forums and communities with caution, recognizing that not all online interactions are positive or supportive. It's vital to prioritize platforms with active moderation, clear guidelines for respectful communication, and mechanisms for reporting inappropriate behavior. Some platforms utilize peer support models, where trained moderators guide discussions, ensuring a safe and supportive environment. Others employ a more informal approach, relying on community members to establish and maintain a respectful atmosphere. Before participating in any online forum or community, it's advisable to review their guidelines and familiarize oneself with their moderation practices. This proactive approach can help minimize exposure to potentially harmful or triggering content.

The availability of online resources presents both opportunities and challenges. While these tools can enhance the therapeutic process and provide valuable support, they require careful selection and mindful utilization. Always prioritize reliable, evidence-based resources, and remember that online tools should complement, not replace, professional therapeutic interventions. A comprehensive approach combining professional guidance with self-directed learning and peer support often yields the most effective outcomes in trauma recovery. This integrated approach allows for personalized support tailored to individual needs, while also providing opportunities for connection and shared experience within a wider community. The judicious use of online resources can thus significantly enhance the overall therapeutic journey.

Beyond the specific apps and websites, there are other digital tools that can indirectly support trauma recovery. For example, using technology to maintain routines and structure can help regulate emotions and improve stability. Setting reminders for medication, therapy appointments, or self-care activities through calendar apps or smartphone reminders can significantly aid in consistency and reduce feelings of overwhelm. Technology can also help in connecting with support systems; scheduling virtual calls with friends, family, or support group members can maintain valuable connections despite geographical distance or scheduling constraints.

The internet also allows access to educational resources that provide information on various aspects of trauma and its effects. Learning about different types of trauma, their potential impact on individuals, and various treatment modalities can aid in self-understanding and empower individuals to make informed decisions about their care. This knowledge can also facilitate conversations with therapists, allowing for more effective collaboration in developing personalized treatment plans. However, it is crucial to remember that self-diagnosing based solely on online information is not advisable. Online research should serve as a starting point for learning and understanding, but professional diagnosis and treatment are essential for effective recovery. The goal should be to enhance self-awareness and facilitate effective communication with healthcare providers, not to replace professional guidance.

In conclusion, while the online world offers a vast array of resources for trauma recovery, a discerning and cautious approach is essential. Careful selection of resources, mindful usage, and integration with professional therapeutic interventions are crucial for maximizing the benefits while minimizing potential risks. By combining the personalized attention of therapy with the convenience and accessibility of online tools and the shared experience of online support communities, individuals can craft a comprehensive and effective path towards healing and lasting well-being. The journey towards recovery is a deeply personal one, and a multimodal approach, integrating various tools and resources, often provides the most supportive and effective pathway to resilience and lasting mental health. Remember that seeking support, whether through online resources or in-person connections, is a sign of strength, not weakness, and is an integral part of the healing process.

Chapter 8: Reclaiming Your Future

Having navigated the challenging terrain of trauma and begun the process of healing, it's now time to turn our gaze towards the future. This isn't about forgetting the past; rather, it's about reclaiming your narrative and actively shaping a life that reflects your strengths, resilience, and aspirations. This involves envisioning a positive future and setting realistic goals that will guide your journey toward well-being and fulfillment. The process of goal setting itself can be therapeutic, providing a sense of agency and control, countering the feelings of helplessness that often accompany trauma.

One of the most effective frameworks for goal setting is the SMART method: Specific, Measurable, Achievable, Relevant, and Time-bound. Let's examine each element in detail, illustrating its application with practical examples relevant to trauma recovery.

Specific: A specific goal leaves no room for ambiguity. Instead of a vague goal like "improve mental health," a specific goal might be "practice mindfulness meditation for 15 minutes daily." Similarly, instead of "eat healthier," a specific goal might be "consume five servings of fruits and vegetables each day." Specificity provides clarity and direction, making it easier to track progress and stay motivated. Think about areas in your life where you'd like to see positive change – relationships, career, physical health, creative pursuits – and articulate them precisely. For example, if your trauma has impacted your ability to trust others, a specific goal might be "engage in one meaningful conversation per week with a trusted friend or family member."

Measurable: A measurable goal allows you to track your progress objectively. You need a clear metric to gauge your success. For the mindfulness meditation example, the measure could be the number of days you successfully practice or the total duration of meditation. For the healthy eating goal, it could be counting the number of fruit and vegetable servings consumed daily. For the goal of improving trust in relationships, you might measure progress by noting instances where you felt comfortable sharing your feelings or trusting another person's actions. Regularly tracking your progress, whether through journaling, a tracking app, or a simple spreadsheet, will reinforce your commitment and offer a visual representation of your achievements.

Achievable: While it's essential to set ambitious goals, it's equally important that they are realistic and achievable within your current capabilities. Starting small and gradually increasing your challenges is often more effective than attempting overly ambitious goals that may lead to discouragement. For instance, if you've experienced social anxiety as a result of trauma, aiming to attend a large social gathering immediately might be unrealistic. Instead, a more achievable goal might be to have a brief conversation with a stranger once a week, perhaps starting with simple interactions like asking for directions or commenting on the weather. Gradually increasing the duration and complexity of these interactions would lead to more significant progress.

Relevant: Your goals should be relevant to your overall well-being and aligned with your values and priorities. Goals that are irrelevant or incongruent with your life's direction are less likely to be sustained. For example, if your primary goal is to improve your emotional regulation, learning a new language might be less relevant than participating in a yoga class or attending anger management workshops. This doesn't mean you should entirely abandon other aspirations, but prioritize goals that directly address your trauma-related challenges and contribute to a more fulfilling and balanced life. Consider what truly matters to you and ensure your goals reflect those values.

Time-bound: Setting a deadline for each goal adds urgency and structure. It helps you break down larger goals into smaller, manageable steps and fosters a sense of accomplishment as you reach intermediate milestones. For the mindfulness meditation example, you might set a goal of practicing daily for one month. For the healthy eating goal, you might set weekly targets for fruit and vegetable consumption. For improving trust in relationships, you might set a monthly goal for the number of meaningful conversations. These deadlines provide a framework for monitoring progress and making necessary adjustments along the way.

Consider these additional points as you develop your SMART goals:

Break down large goals: Divide larger, more complex goals into smaller, more manageable steps. This helps prevent overwhelm and maintain momentum. For example, if your goal is to return to work after a trauma-induced break, you might break it down into smaller steps such as researching suitable positions, updating your resume, practicing interview skills, and attending networking events.

Celebrate milestones: Acknowledge and celebrate your achievements, no matter how small. This positive reinforcement boosts morale and motivation, keeping you engaged throughout the process. Celebrate the small wins – a completed meditation session, a healthy meal, a successful conversation.

Allow for flexibility: Life is unpredictable, and setbacks are inevitable. It's crucial to allow for flexibility in your goals. Don't be discouraged by setbacks; view them as opportunities to learn and adjust your approach. If you miss a meditation session, simply resume your practice the next day without self-criticism.

Seek support: Share your goals with a trusted friend, family member, therapist, or support group. Their encouragement and accountability can be invaluable in maintaining motivation and navigating challenges. They can also offer practical advice and guidance based on their own experiences.

Re-evaluate and adjust: Regularly review your progress and make adjustments as needed. Your goals should evolve along with your healing journey. What was challenging six months ago might be easier now, and new goals may emerge as you grow and develop.

The process of setting goals is an ongoing one, a dynamic interaction between your aspirations and your evolving capabilities. It's a journey of self-discovery and empowerment, where you are actively shaping your future, rather than passively reacting to your past. By setting SMART goals and actively working towards them, you are not only reclaiming your future but also building resilience and strengthening your capacity for self-compassion and self-care. Remember, this is your journey, and your progress is your own to define. The crucial aspect is the continuous striving towards a future defined by your own terms and filled with hope and well-being.

Building upon the foundation of SMART goal-setting, we now move towards a crucial element of reclaiming your future: developing a compelling vision for your life. This isn't merely about setting individual goals; it's about weaving those goals into a cohesive narrative of your ideal future, a future reflecting your values, aspirations, and the person you envision becoming. This vision acts as a guiding star, illuminating your path and motivating you through challenges.

This process begins with introspection. Take some quiet time, free from distractions, and consider the following questions: What kind of relationships do you want to cultivate? Do you envision close, intimate bonds, a wider network of friends, or a combination of both? What kind of work brings you fulfillment? What are your passions and talents, and how can you integrate them into your daily life? What kind of physical and mental well-being do you strive for? How do you want to spend your leisure time? What kind of contribution do you want to make to the world? These questions are a starting point; allow yourself to explore the nuances of your aspirations without judgment. Write down your responses, even if they seem uncertain or unrealistic at this stage. This act of articulation is transformative.

One effective technique for envisioning your future is visualization. Find a quiet, comfortable space where you can relax and close your eyes. Engage your senses. Imagine yourself in your ideal future. What do you see around you? What are you doing? Who are you with? What emotions are you feeling? Pay attention to the details: the sounds you hear, the smells in the air, the tastes you experience, the textures you feel. Make this vision as vivid and compelling as possible. The more sensory detail you incorporate, the more powerful the visualization will be. This isn't about creating a fantasy; it's about consciously crafting a future aligned with your deepest values and aspirations.

Visualization can be used in various contexts. You can practice it daily for a few minutes, using it as a form of meditation. You can also incorporate it into your goal-setting process, visualizing yourself achieving specific milestones along the way. For instance, if your goal is to return to work after a period of trauma-related absence, visualize yourself succeeding in an interview, comfortable and confident in your abilities. Visualize yourself interacting positively with colleagues, feeling a sense of accomplishment and purpose in your work. This process strengthens your belief in your ability to achieve your goals and reduces the feelings of anxiety or doubt that may arise.

Remember, this vision is a work in progress, constantly evolving and refining itself as you grow and develop. It's not meant to be a rigid plan etched in stone; rather, it's a flexible guideline, adapting to the unexpected turns and challenges life throws your way. Regularly revisit your vision; update it as you progress and adjust your goals. This ongoing process reinforces your commitment and allows you to maintain a sense of purpose and direction even amidst inevitable setbacks.

Let's delve deeper into various aspects of your future vision. Consider your relationships. Do you desire deeper connections with existing relationships or build new ones? If it's the former, identify specific steps you can take to nurture these bonds. This might include scheduling regular time for meaningful conversations, actively listening to your loved ones, expressing your appreciation, and showing empathy. If you wish to cultivate new relationships, consider joining social groups aligned with your interests, attending workshops or courses, or volunteering your time for a cause you care about.

In terms of your career, what kind of work truly excites and motivates you? Is it a specific career path, or is it more about the type of environment or the impact you wish to create? If your trauma has impacted your career trajectory, consider career counseling or coaching to help you navigate your options and identify opportunities that align with your skills and aspirations. Explore professional development opportunities, such as workshops, online courses, or further education, to enhance your capabilities and broaden your prospects. Remember to celebrate small victories along the way, such as completing a course or successfully applying for a job. These achievements bolster your self-confidence and reinforce your belief in your ability to achieve your goals.

Your vision also encompasses your personal aspirations. What are your passions and hobbies? How can you dedicate more time to activities that bring you joy and fulfillment? This might involve joining a sports club, taking up a creative pursuit like painting or writing, learning a new language, or simply spending more time in nature. These activities aren't just diversions; they're essential elements of a balanced and fulfilling life. They promote mental and physical well-being, providing opportunities for stress reduction, self-expression, and social connection.

Physical and mental health are paramount. Your vision should incorporate strategies to maintain and enhance both. This might involve incorporating regular exercise into your routine, adopting a healthy diet, practicing mindfulness or meditation, engaging in relaxation techniques, and seeking professional support when needed. It's about making conscious choices that prioritize your overall well-being, not just as a means to an end, but as integral parts of a life rich in purpose and joy.

Finally, consider the contribution you want to make to the world. What causes are meaningful to you? How can you use your skills and talents to create a positive impact? This could range from volunteering your time to a local charity to advocating for social justice or pursuing a career that aligns with your values. The act of contributing to something larger than yourself is inherently fulfilling, fostering a sense of purpose and connection.

Remember, this vision is yours to create. There's no right or wrong way to envision your future. The process itself is transformative, empowering you to take control of your narrative and shape a life that truly reflects your values and aspirations. By integrating your goals into a coherent vision and regularly revisiting and updating it, you actively participate in the construction of your future, transforming from a survivor of trauma to a thriving, empowered individual. This journey of self-discovery and creation is ongoing, a testament to your resilience and the unwavering strength of your spirit. Embrace this journey, celebrate your progress, and allow your vision to guide you toward a life filled with hope, purpose, and well-being. The future you envision is attainable, and the path to get there is paved with your own determination and the support you seek and find along the way.

The process of envisioning your future, while empowering, can also unearth anxieties and fears, especially for those who have experienced trauma. The past, with its painful memories and lingering effects, can cast a long shadow, making it difficult to imagine a brighter future. Fear of repeating past traumas, of experiencing further setbacks, or simply of the unknown can paralyze us, preventing us from embracing the possibilities that lie ahead. This fear is a valid response to trauma, but it doesn't have to define your future.

Understanding the source of this fear is the first step towards overcoming it. Trauma often leaves us feeling vulnerable and uncertain, making us anticipate potential threats and dangers. This hypervigilance, while a survival mechanism in the past, can become a significant obstacle to building a positive future. It might manifest as intrusive thoughts about potential harm, persistent worries about the future, or an inability to let go of the past. Recognizing that these fears are rooted in your past trauma is crucial – it's not a sign of weakness, but rather a testament to your resilience in the face of adversity.

To manage these fears effectively, we need to employ a multi-pronged approach that combines cognitive strategies with somatic and mindfulness techniques. Cognitive restructuring, a cornerstone of trauma-informed therapy, involves challenging negative and catastrophic thoughts about the future. When faced with anxieties, ask yourself: Is this thought realistic? What evidence supports this thought? What alternative explanations are possible? Are my fears proportional to the actual likelihood of the event? By systematically questioning your negative thoughts, you can dismantle their power and replace them with more balanced and optimistic perspectives.

Mindfulness practices are invaluable in calming the nervous system and reducing the intensity of fear responses. Mindful breathing exercises, for example, can help ground you in the present moment, reducing the grip of anxious thoughts about the future. Focusing on your breath – the sensation of the air entering and leaving your body – can anchor you to the present, providing a sense of stability and calm amidst feelings of uncertainty. Mindful body scans, which involve systematically bringing awareness to different parts of your body, can help you connect with your physical sensations, becoming more attuned to your body's signals and better able to regulate emotional responses.

Somatic practices, which focus on the body's experience of trauma, are particularly helpful in addressing the physical manifestations of fear. Trauma is often stored in the body, leading to physical tension, chronic pain, or other somatic symptoms. Somatic experiencing, a form of therapy that helps you process trauma through body awareness, can facilitate the release of trapped energy and alleviate physical symptoms associated with fear and anxiety. Gentle movement practices like yoga, tai chi, or qigong can also help release tension and promote a sense of calm and groundedness. These practices aren't about pushing through discomfort, but rather about gently moving your body in a way that feels safe and supportive.

Another crucial aspect of overcoming fear of the future is building self-compassion. Be kind to yourself; recognize that it's normal to feel fear and anxiety, especially after experiencing trauma. Don't judge yourself harshly for having these feelings. Instead, acknowledge them with acceptance and understanding. Treat yourself with the same kindness and empathy you would offer a friend in a similar situation. Self-compassion helps to reduce self-criticism, fostering a sense of self-worth and resilience.

Developing a strong support system is also vital. Share your fears and anxieties with trusted friends, family members, or a therapist. Talking about your experiences can help you process your emotions, gain perspective, and feel less alone. A supportive community can provide you with encouragement, practical assistance, and a sense of belonging. Remember that you are not alone in this journey; seeking and accepting support is a sign of strength, not weakness.

Alongside these coping strategies, actively working towards your goals, as outlined in the previous sections, is crucial in building confidence and hope. Each step you take towards achieving your goals, no matter how small, reinforces your belief in your ability to create a positive future. Celebrate your accomplishments, acknowledging your efforts and resilience. This positive reinforcement helps to counteract negative thoughts and anxieties, building momentum and fostering a sense of agency.

Visualizing your ideal future, as we discussed earlier, is not just about creating a mental image; it's also about cultivating a sense of hope and possibility. By regularly engaging in visualization, you strengthen your belief in your ability to achieve your aspirations. This doesn't mean ignoring the challenges that lie ahead; rather, it's about cultivating a mindset of optimism and resilience, approaching difficulties with a sense of determination and confidence in your ability to overcome them.

It's important to remember that the future is not predetermined. While we cannot control every aspect of our lives, we can influence our trajectory by making conscious choices and actively working towards our goals. Embrace the uncertainty; see it not as a threat, but as an opportunity for growth and discovery. The future is a canvas upon which you can paint your own masterpiece, a reflection of your values, aspirations, and resilience. This journey of creating your future is a testament to your strength, a journey of healing and empowerment.

Remember that setbacks are inevitable. There will be times when you face challenges and obstacles, and it's okay to feel discouraged or overwhelmed. These moments are opportunities for learning and growth. View them as temporary setbacks, not as definitive failures. Reflect on what you've learned from these experiences, adjust your approach if necessary, and continue moving forward. The path to creating a positive future is rarely linear; it's a journey of continuous growth and adaptation.

Cultivate patience and self-compassion. Healing from trauma takes time, and creating a fulfilling future is a process, not a destination. Be kind to yourself, acknowledge your progress, and celebrate your successes along the way. Every step you take is a step towards reclaiming your future, towards creating a life that reflects your values and aspirations. This journey requires courage, resilience, and a unwavering belief in your own ability to create a brighter tomorrow.

Don't hesitate to seek professional help if you find yourself struggling. A therapist specializing in trauma and stress management can provide you with the support and guidance you need to navigate your fears and build a resilient future. Therapy offers a safe and supportive space to process your experiences, develop coping skills, and work towards your goals. Remember that seeking help is a sign of strength, not weakness. It demonstrates your commitment to your well-being and your determination to create a positive and fulfilling future. You deserve to live a life free from the constraints of your past, a life filled with hope, purpose, and joy. The future you envision is within your reach, and with consistent effort and support, you can create a life that truly reflects your values and aspirations. The journey may be challenging, but the destination – a future filled with hope and resilience – is worth the effort. Believe in yourself, trust your strength, and embrace the journey.

Building a strong sense of self-esteem and confidence is paramount to reclaiming your future after trauma. It's a fundamental building block for navigating challenges, setting goals, and ultimately, achieving a life filled with purpose and joy. Trauma often erodes self-worth, leaving individuals feeling vulnerable and uncertain about their capabilities. However, rebuilding self-esteem is entirely possible, and this section will guide you through practical strategies to achieve this vital goal.

The first step in building self-esteem involves identifying your personal strengths. This might seem challenging initially, particularly if you've internalized negative self-perceptions due to past experiences. Take some time for self-reflection. Consider past situations where you felt competent, resourceful, or resilient. Perhaps you successfully navigated a difficult relationship, overcame a significant obstacle, or demonstrated exceptional empathy towards someone in need. These moments, however small they may seem, highlight your inherent strengths and capabilities.

To facilitate this process, try journaling. Write down specific instances where you exhibited resilience, problem-solving skills, creativity, or compassion. Don't downplay your achievements; even seemingly minor successes are worthy of acknowledgment. For example, if you consistently overcame procrastination to complete a challenging task, this showcases discipline and self-efficacy. If you successfully navigated a conflict with grace and understanding, this highlights your emotional intelligence and ability to manage difficult situations. If you cared for a sick family member, this underscores your empathy and dedication. Documenting these instances will create a tangible record of your accomplishments, strengthening your self-perception.

Once you've identified several instances that highlight your strengths, reflect on the qualities that were demonstrated. Are you resourceful? Empathetic? Persistent? Creative? Organized? This process of identifying and naming your strengths is crucial for building self-esteem. It shifts the focus from your perceived weaknesses or past failures to your inherent capabilities and positive qualities. This is not about boasting or self-aggrandizement; it's about cultivating a realistic and balanced view of yourself, recognizing both your strengths and areas where you might benefit from further development.

After identifying your strengths, the next step is to celebrate your achievements. This goes beyond simply acknowledging your successes; it involves actively celebrating and appreciating your accomplishments, both large and small. Society often emphasizes grand achievements, making it easy to overlook the significance of daily triumphs. However, these small wins accumulate to contribute significantly to our overall sense of accomplishment and self-efficacy. Make a conscious effort to acknowledge and celebrate every milestone you reach, no matter how seemingly insignificant. Did you complete a challenging workout? Did you finally tackle that daunting task you'd been putting off? Did you maintain a healthy lifestyle choice for a week? Each of these achievements, while seemingly minor in isolation, contributes to a broader sense of self-efficacy and competence.

To further reinforce this practice, consider creating a "success journal."

In this journal, document your achievements, both big and small. Include specific details about the accomplishment, how you felt during and after the achievement, and the lessons you learned from the experience. This journal serves as a tangible record of your progress, reminding you of your capabilities and strengthening your self-belief. Review this journal regularly to reinforce your sense of accomplishment and to identify patterns of success, which can guide your future endeavors. This constant reinforcement of your positive qualities and achievements is crucial in building lasting self-esteem.

Another critical element in building self-esteem is practicing self-compassion. This involves treating yourself with the same kindness, understanding, and empathy you would offer a close friend struggling with similar challenges. Trauma often leaves individuals prone to self-criticism and harsh self-judgment. Counteracting this tendency is essential for building resilience and self-worth. When you encounter setbacks or make mistakes, resist the urge to engage in self-flagellation. Instead, acknowledge your feelings, acknowledge the situation, and treat yourself with compassion. Remind yourself that mistakes are opportunities for learning and growth, not evidence of personal failure.

Cultivating self-compassion involves several key practices. First, recognize that you are not alone in your struggles. Many people experience similar challenges, and it's completely normal to feel overwhelmed or discouraged at times. Second, treat yourself with kindness and understanding. Avoid harsh self-criticism; instead, offer yourself words of encouragement and support. Third, acknowledge that your experience is valid and worthy of compassion. Avoid minimizing your feelings or dismissing your suffering. Finally, remind yourself that you are worthy of love and acceptance, regardless of your mistakes or shortcomings.

Practicing self-compassion is an ongoing process, not a one-time event. It requires consistent effort and self-awareness. It involves paying attention to your inner dialogue and challenging negative self-talk. When you notice yourself engaging in self-criticism, gently redirect your thoughts towards self-acceptance and understanding. Self-compassion involves recognizing your imperfections and accepting them without judgment.

This self-compassionate approach extends to the challenges you encounter in working towards your goals. Remember that setbacks are a natural part of any growth process. Don't let occasional stumbles derail your progress. Instead, approach setbacks as opportunities for learning and growth. Reflect on what went wrong, adjust your strategy as needed, and continue moving forward. Celebrate small victories along the way, acknowledging your resilience and perseverance.

Furthermore, visualize your future self as someone confident and self-assured. Imagine yourself effortlessly tackling challenges, pursuing your goals with determination, and experiencing the joy and fulfillment that comes from living a life aligned with your values. This mental exercise can be a powerful tool for building self-esteem and confidence, helping you bridge the gap between your current self and your envisioned future self. Regularly engaging in this visualization exercise reinforces your belief in your ability to achieve your aspirations.

Finally, remember that building self-esteem and confidence is a journey, not a destination. It requires consistent effort, self-awareness, and self-compassion. There will be ups and downs, setbacks and triumphs. The key is to remain committed to the process, celebrating your progress along the way, and learning from your experiences. Be patient with yourself, acknowledge your strengths, and celebrate your achievements. The path to reclaiming your future is paved with self-belief, and each step you take, however small, brings you closer to the life you envision. Believe in yourself; you have the strength and resilience to create the future you desire.

Building a strong foundation of self-esteem and confidence is crucial, but it's only one piece of the puzzle. True reclamation of your future after trauma involves embracing a deeper level of self-acceptance and self-love. This isn't about superficial positivity or ignoring your struggles; it's about cultivating a profound understanding and appreciation of your whole self – flaws, strengths, and all. It's about recognizing your inherent worthiness, regardless of past experiences or perceived imperfections.

This journey begins with acknowledging that self-acceptance isn't a destination, but a continuous process. It's a daily practice, a conscious choice to treat yourself with kindness and understanding, especially during moments of vulnerability or self-doubt. It requires actively challenging the negative self-talk and limiting beliefs that trauma may have instilled. Remember, your worth isn't contingent upon external validation or achievement. Your value is intrinsic; it's inherent to your being.

One powerful tool for fostering self-acceptance is practicing radical self-acceptance. This involves accepting all aspects of yourself without judgment – the parts you love and the parts you find challenging. It requires recognizing that your past experiences don't define your entire being. You are not your trauma; you are so much more than the sum of your difficult experiences. You are resilient, you are capable, and you are worthy of love and compassion, irrespective of past mistakes or perceived failures.

Radical self-acceptance necessitates a willingness to be vulnerable and honest with yourself. This may involve confronting difficult emotions and memories, but it also requires recognizing the courage and strength it takes to face those challenges. It's about acknowledging your imperfections, not as flaws to be eradicated, but as integral parts of your unique story. Embrace your quirks, your vulnerabilities, and your imperfections; they are what make you, you. They are a testament to your journey, your resilience, and your humanity.

To further cultivate radical self-acceptance, consider creating a list of your qualities – both positive and negative. Don't shy away from the challenging aspects; acknowledge them honestly and without judgment. Then, alongside each negative attribute, write down counterbalancing positive qualities or strengths. For example, if you list "impatience" as a negative trait, you might balance it with "passionate" or "driven." If "perfectionism" is a challenge, balance it with "meticulous" or "highly organized." This exercise helps you see a more balanced and realistic picture of yourself, fostering self-compassion and acceptance.

Beyond radical self-acceptance lies the cultivation of self-love. Self-love is not ego-centric or narcissistic; it's a deep, abiding respect and compassion for yourself. It's about prioritizing your well-being, setting healthy boundaries, and actively nurturing your emotional and physical health. It involves making choices that align with your values and contribute to your overall happiness and well-being. It's recognizing that you deserve to be treated with kindness, respect, and compassion, just as you would treat someone you love dearly.

One crucial element of self-love is engaging in activities that bring you joy and fulfillment. This might involve pursuing hobbies, spending time in nature, connecting with loved ones, or simply relaxing and engaging in self-care practices. These activities nourish your soul, reminding you of the beauty and richness of life, even amidst challenges. They provide opportunities to reconnect with your inner self and nurture your emotional well-being. Prioritizing self-care is not selfish; it's essential for your overall health and well-being.

Another aspect of self-love is learning to forgive yourself. Trauma often involves self-blame and self-criticism. Forgiving yourself for past actions or choices is a crucial step towards healing and self-acceptance. It's not about condoning harmful behaviors, but rather about releasing the burden of guilt and self-reproach. Recognize that you did the best you could with the resources and understanding you had at the time. Forgiveness paves the way for healing and growth, allowing you to move forward with renewed purpose and compassion.

Consider practicing self-compassion meditation. These guided meditations often involve focusing on your breath and gently acknowledging your thoughts and feelings without judgment. They can help you cultivate a sense of inner peace and acceptance, fostering self-love and compassion. Many apps and online resources offer guided self-compassion meditations that can be incorporated into your daily routine. Even just a few minutes of daily practice can significantly impact your emotional well-being.

Engage in positive self-affirmations. These are positive statements that reinforce your self-worth and self-acceptance. They can help to counteract negative self-talk and promote a more positive self-image. Examples include: "I am worthy of love and acceptance," "I am capable and strong," "I am resilient and resourceful," "I am enough." Repeat these affirmations daily, ideally in front of a mirror, to reinforce their message and strengthen your belief in yourself.

Journaling can be a powerful tool for processing emotions and promoting self-understanding. Use your journal to explore your thoughts and feelings about self-acceptance and self-love. Write about your strengths, your challenges, and your progress. Reflect on your experiences and identify patterns of self-criticism or self-doubt. This process can help you develop a deeper understanding of yourself and foster self-compassion.

Remember, self-acceptance and self-love are ongoing journeys, not destinations. There will be days when you struggle, days when self-doubt creeps in. This is normal; it's part of the human experience. The key is to be kind to yourself during these moments, to offer yourself the same compassion and understanding you would offer a loved one. Celebrate your progress, no matter how small. Acknowledge your efforts and resilience. You are worthy of a life filled with joy, purpose, and self-acceptance. Embrace the journey, and believe in your capacity for healing and growth. The future you reclaim will be one built on a foundation of self-love and self-acceptance. This is not a passive process; it requires consistent effort, self-reflection, and a commitment to nurturing your inner world. Be patient, be kind, and believe in the incredible power of self-compassion.

Chapter 9: Maintaining Progress and Preventing Relapse

Maintaining progress after trauma is a dynamic process, not a static achievement. While building self-esteem and self-love forms a crucial foundation, the journey toward lasting healing necessitates understanding and proactively addressing potential triggers and challenges that might derail your progress. Relapse isn't a sign of failure; rather, it's an opportunity to refine your coping mechanisms and strengthen your resilience. Recognizing this reality empowers you to approach setbacks with a sense of agency and control.

The first step in preventing relapse is identifying potential triggers. These can be internal or external stimuli that evoke strong emotional responses, potentially overwhelming your coping mechanisms and leading you back into patterns of negative thinking or behavior. Internal triggers might include specific thoughts, memories, or emotions. For instance, a sudden wave of intense self-criticism, a vivid flashback, or an overwhelming sense of anxiety could serve as internal triggers, pushing you toward unhealthy coping strategies like substance use, isolation, or self-harm. Recognizing these internal triggers requires keen self-awareness and honest self-reflection. Journaling can be an invaluable tool here, allowing you to track your emotional state and identify patterns or connections between specific thoughts, feelings, and subsequent behaviors. Regular self-reflection, even brief moments of mindfulness throughout the day, can increase your capacity to identify these internal cues before they escalate into a full-blown relapse.

External triggers are stimuli from your environment that can evoke strong reactions. These may include specific people, places, situations, or even sensory experiences. The sight of a particular object, a sound, a smell, or even a certain type of weather can trigger intense emotional responses, especially if associated with past traumatic events. For example, a person who experienced a car accident might experience anxiety and panic when driving past the location of the accident or even when simply hearing the sound of screeching brakes. Similarly, exposure to certain people – such as individuals who remind you of the person who harmed you – can reactivate past trauma. Recognizing these external triggers involves being mindful of your surroundings and noting any patterns that seem to consistently precede periods of distress or emotional upheaval.

Once you have identified your potential triggers, both internal and external, the next crucial step is developing personalized coping strategies. These strategies should be tailored to your individual needs and preferences, ensuring they are readily accessible and practical for your daily life. For example, if a particular memory consistently triggers intense anxiety, you might develop a coping strategy that involves practicing mindfulness techniques like deep breathing exercises or progressive muscle relaxation. These techniques can help ground you in the present moment, reducing the intensity of the emotional response. If social situations trigger feelings of vulnerability or overwhelming anxiety, you might develop strategies that include limiting exposure to triggering situations, or practicing assertiveness techniques to set boundaries and protect your emotional well-being. If certain physical sensations – such as a racing heart – serve as a trigger, you might practice grounding techniques such as focusing on your physical senses or engaging in physical activities that help regulate your nervous system, like yoga or tai chi.

It's vital to develop a range of coping strategies, catering to different situations and emotional states. A multifaceted approach enhances your ability to effectively manage various challenges. One strategy might be effective in one situation but not in another. For instance, while deep breathing may help manage anxiety during a stressful work meeting, it may not be sufficient to cope with a sudden flashback of a traumatic event. In such instances, a more comprehensive approach might involve a combination of grounding techniques, emotional regulation strategies, and seeking support from a trusted friend, family member, or therapist.

The development of coping strategies should be an ongoing process. It's not enough to simply create a list; you need to actively practice and refine your strategies over time. This requires patience, persistence, and a willingness to adapt as needed. Regularly reviewing and adjusting your coping strategies allows you to refine your approach, ensuring that they remain relevant and effective as you progress through your healing journey. The effectiveness of your coping strategies can be evaluated by tracking your emotional responses to triggers. You might track your mood, stress levels, and any other relevant variables over a period of time, noting which strategies proved most effective in managing various situations.

Moreover, building a strong support system is essential for preventing relapse. This support system should include individuals who understand your experiences and can offer empathy, encouragement, and practical assistance during difficult times. This might involve family members, friends, support groups, or a mental health professional. Regularly connecting with your support network can provide a sense of community, reduce feelings of isolation, and enhance your ability to cope with challenging situations. These individuals can offer a safe space for emotional expression, practical assistance, or simply a listening ear.

In addition to building a strong support network, it is crucial to proactively manage stress. Stress can exacerbate the effects of trauma and increase the likelihood of relapse. Effective stress management techniques can significantly improve your ability to manage stressful situations and prevent them from escalating into a crisis. These techniques can include various self-care practices such as regular exercise, adequate sleep, a healthy diet, and engaging in activities that you enjoy and find relaxing. The incorporation of mindfulness techniques into your daily routine can also significantly reduce stress levels and enhance your emotional regulation skills.

Remember, relapse prevention is an ongoing process, and setbacks are inevitable. If you experience a relapse, it's important not to get discouraged. Treat it as a learning opportunity, analyze what triggered the relapse, and adjust your coping mechanisms as needed. Seek support from your therapist, support group, or trusted individuals. Maintain self-compassion during these times and remind yourself that you are not defined by your setbacks. The key is to learn from your experiences, build resilience, and move forward with renewed determination.

The journey to lasting recovery from trauma is a marathon, not a sprint. It requires consistent effort, self-awareness, and a proactive approach to managing challenges. By identifying potential triggers, developing and refining coping strategies, building a strong support system, and proactively managing stress, you can significantly reduce the risk of relapse and build a stronger, more resilient self. This continuous work builds a foundation of self-compassion, fostering self-acceptance and empowering you to navigate future challenges with grace and strength. It's a testament to your unwavering commitment to your own well-being and your inherent capacity for growth and healing. Remember that seeking professional help is not a sign of weakness but a demonstration of your strength and commitment to your healing journey. Your mental health provider can work collaboratively with you, providing guidance, support, and tailored strategies for managing your unique challenges. This collaborative approach fosters empowerment and a deeper understanding of your strengths and resources, paving the way for lasting healing and recovery.

Developing a comprehensive relapse prevention plan is crucial for maintaining progress and preventing a return to unhealthy coping mechanisms after trauma. This plan isn't a rigid set of rules, but rather a flexible, personalized roadmap guiding you through potential challenges. Think of it as a proactive tool, equipping you with strategies to navigate difficult moments and maintain your hard-earned progress. The process involves several key steps, and the effectiveness of your plan will depend on your consistent engagement and willingness to adapt as needed.

The first step is

identifying your high-risk situations. These are specific circumstances, internal states, or external environments that have historically triggered negative behaviors or emotional distress. We've already discussed identifying internal triggers like negative self-talk, overwhelming anxiety, or specific memories. Now, let's delve deeper into refining this identification process. Consider keeping a detailed journal, noting not only the emotional experience but also the context surrounding it: Where were you? Who were you with? What were you doing? What specific thoughts preceded the negative feelings? This detailed analysis can reveal subtle patterns that might otherwise go unnoticed. For example, you might discover that feelings of loneliness often precede unhealthy coping mechanisms, highlighting the importance of proactive social engagement in your relapse prevention plan.

Similarly, examining your external triggers requires thorough self-reflection. Beyond obvious triggers like specific places or people, consider less obvious factors such as weather patterns, certain smells, or even specific times of day. These subtle triggers can be surprisingly powerful. One individual, for example, might discover that the onset of winter, with its shorter days and colder weather, triggers feelings of depression and isolation. Another might find that the aroma of freshly baked bread, reminiscent of a childhood trauma, evokes overwhelming anxiety. Understanding these subtle cues is essential for creating a truly effective relapse prevention plan.

The next critical step is

developing specific coping strategies. These aren't generic solutions; they need to be tailored to your unique triggers and vulnerabilities. Consider creating a "coping skills toolbox," a readily accessible list of specific strategies for different situations. For instance, if feelings of loneliness are a significant trigger, your toolbox might include scheduling regular calls with supportive friends, joining a community group, or engaging in online forums with shared interests. For individuals triggered by specific memories, the toolbox might contain mindfulness exercises, progressive muscle relaxation techniques, or guided imagery. If a particular place or situation is a trigger, you might include strategies for avoiding it, or preparing yourself mentally and emotionally before exposure.

Your coping strategies should encompass various approaches to address different aspects of your well-being. This might include:

Mindfulness and somatic practices: Techniques like deep breathing, body scans, and yoga can help regulate your nervous system and manage overwhelming emotions.

Cognitive restructuring: This involves challenging and reframing negative or unhelpful thought patterns. For example, if you find yourself thinking "I'm a failure," you might reframe this thought to "I'm facing a challenge, and I have the strength to overcome it."

Emotional regulation techniques: Learning to identify and manage your emotions is crucial. This might include techniques like journaling, expressive writing, or engaging in creative activities.

Social support: Connecting with supportive friends, family, or support groups can provide a sense of belonging and reduce feelings of isolation.

Self-care practices: Prioritizing activities that nourish your physical and emotional well-being, such as exercise, healthy eating, and adequate sleep.

Remember, the strategies in your toolbox need to be easily accessible and practical for your daily life. Don't overwhelm yourself with complex techniques you won't utilize. Simplicity and accessibility are key to their effectiveness. Regularly review and update your toolbox, adding new strategies or refining existing ones based on your experiences.

Next, we'll focus on

building a strong support system. This involves identifying individuals who understand your journey and can offer unconditional support. This could include family members, friends, therapists, support groups, or even online communities. It's crucial to have individuals who can offer empathetic listening, practical assistance, and encouragement during challenging moments. Your support network should be diverse, providing different types of support depending on your needs. Some people may offer emotional support, while others may offer practical help with daily tasks. Regularly connecting with your support system can significantly enhance your resilience and ability to cope with stressful situations.

Effective stress management is another cornerstone of relapse prevention. Stress can significantly increase the risk of relapse, so proactively addressing stress is essential. Incorporate stress-reducing activities into your daily routine, such as regular exercise, mindfulness meditation, yoga, spending time in nature, or engaging in hobbies you enjoy. Prioritizing sleep, maintaining a healthy diet, and setting healthy boundaries are also vital for managing stress effectively. Identify your personal stress triggers and develop strategies to manage or avoid them. This might involve setting realistic expectations, learning to say "no," or delegating tasks.

The

creation of a written relapse prevention plan is a powerful step. This is not just a mental exercise, but a tangible document that serves as a guide and reminder during challenging moments. Your plan should include:

A list of your identified high-risk situations, both internal and external.

A detailed description of your coping skills toolbox, outlining specific strategies for each trigger.

Contact information for your support network, including therapists, friends, and family members.

A schedule for your self-care activities, such as exercise, mindfulness practices, and other stress-reducing activities.

A plan for what you will do if you experience a relapse, including steps to take and who to contact.

Regularly review and update your relapse prevention plan. This is an ongoing process, and your needs and circumstances will change over time. The plan should be a living document, reflecting your progress and adaptations.

Finally, remember that

relapse is not failure. It's a part of the healing process. If a relapse occurs, don't be discouraged. View it as an opportunity to learn and refine your relapse prevention plan. Analyze the circumstances that led to the relapse, identify any gaps in your coping strategies, and make necessary adjustments. Seek additional support from your therapist or support network. Remember, self-compassion is crucial throughout this process. Be kind to yourself, acknowledge your progress, and continue moving forward with renewed determination. Your journey is unique, and your commitment to recovery is commendable. The consistent effort you put into relapse prevention will build lasting resilience, empowerment, and a stronger, more resilient self.

Building a robust support network is not merely beneficial; it's fundamental to sustained recovery from trauma. This network acts as a crucial buffer against the inevitable challenges that arise during the healing process. It's a lifeline, offering a sense of belonging, understanding, and practical assistance when you need it most. Think of it as a safety net, catching you when you stumble and providing the encouragement to keep moving forward. But building this network requires proactive effort and a willingness to reach out and accept the help offered.

The first step in cultivating a supportive network involves identifying the individuals already present in your life who offer genuine care and understanding. These individuals might be family members, close friends, colleagues, or mentors who have consistently demonstrated empathy and support. It's important to recognize that not everyone in your life is equipped to provide the kind of support you need during this phase of healing. Some relationships may be strained or even toxic, requiring careful consideration and potentially, boundaries.

Assessing your current relationships with honesty and self-compassion is critical. Identify those who consistently listen without judgment, who offer encouragement without minimizing your experience, and who respect your boundaries. These are the individuals who form the foundation of your support network. Then, consider those individuals you'd like to cultivate closer relationships with or who might be good additions to your network. Remember, quality is more important than quantity. A small, dependable group offering genuine support is far more valuable than a large, superficial network that offers little tangible assistance.

Once you've identified potential members of your support network, the next step is fostering these connections. This involves actively engaging with these individuals, sharing your journey with them (to the extent you feel comfortable), and allowing them to provide support in ways that feel meaningful to you. This could involve sharing your experiences, asking for assistance with specific tasks, or simply spending quality time together. Open communication is key. Don't hesitate to express your needs and expectations clearly. Be honest about what type of support you find most helpful—whether it's emotional support, practical assistance, or simply companionship.

Remember that receiving support doesn't mean you're weak or incapable. It's a sign of strength and self-awareness to recognize your need for support and actively seek it out. It's about acknowledging your vulnerability and building resilience by creating a network of individuals who can offer a helping hand when needed. Many find that having a variety of support is the most beneficial. For example, some individuals may offer excellent emotional support, listening with empathy and providing encouragement. Others may be better equipped to offer practical assistance, such as help with chores, errands, or transportation.

Beyond the existing individuals in your life, consider actively seeking out additional sources of support. Support groups, for instance, offer a unique opportunity to connect with others who share similar experiences. These groups provide a safe and non-judgmental space to share your story, receive support, and learn from others' experiences. The sense of community found within these groups can be incredibly powerful, helping to reduce feelings of isolation and shame that often accompany trauma. Online support groups offer additional accessibility and anonymity, especially helpful for those who find it challenging to attend in-person meetings. Many organizations and charities dedicated to trauma recovery offer online forums and communities where you can connect with others and find support. Researching relevant groups based on your specific experiences is highly beneficial. Some might cater to specific types of trauma, while others might offer support based on age, gender, or cultural background.

Furthermore, considering professional support is crucial. A therapist specializing in trauma and stress management can provide valuable guidance and tools to navigate your healing journey. Therapy provides a structured environment for processing trauma, developing coping mechanisms, and addressing underlying psychological issues. Remember that seeking professional help isn't a sign of weakness, but rather a proactive step towards achieving optimal mental well-being. A therapist can guide you through developing effective strategies for managing emotional distress, stress, and relapse prevention. They can offer valuable insights, help to unpack complex emotions, and support you in identifying patterns of thinking and behaving that contribute to your difficulties.

Building a strong support network is an ongoing process, not a one-time event. As your circumstances change and your healing progresses, the nature and composition of your support network may evolve as well. What was helpful a few months ago might not be as effective now. Regularly reassess your network, ensuring it meets your changing needs. Some individuals may fade out of the picture as you progress, while new, more suitable support may emerge. This is a natural part of the healing process. Be prepared to adapt and adjust your support network to ensure it remains a reliable source of strength and resilience.

It's also crucial to actively nurture your relationships within your support network. Just like any relationship, these connections require ongoing effort and maintenance. Regular communication, both scheduled and spontaneous, is essential. This might involve regular phone calls, text messages, emails, or even simply spending time together in person. Remember to show appreciation for the support you receive. Expressing gratitude for the assistance and companionship offered strengthens the bonds within your network and encourages ongoing support.

Furthermore, understanding your own limitations within your support network is important. Don't hesitate to ask for what you need from each individual, but remember to respect their limits as well. Your support network isn't expected to carry your entire burden; they are there to lighten your load, not to bear it alone. Recognizing your personal boundaries and setting healthy expectations will strengthen your support network and foster a healthier relationship with those who help you on your journey.

Remember, relapse prevention is not just about avoiding specific situations or triggers, it's about building resilience and strength. A strong support network significantly enhances your capacity to cope with challenging moments. This network doesn't replace professional help or individual efforts; instead, it serves as a crucial supplement, offering a sense of community, practical assistance, and unconditional support during times of need. Actively cultivating a strong support network is one of the most significant steps towards long-term healing and sustained recovery. The consistent effort in nurturing these connections will be rewarded with increased resilience, empowerment, and a stronger, more resilient self.

The journey of healing from trauma is not a linear path; it's a winding road with ups and downs, twists and turns. While building a strong support network provides invaluable external scaffolding, the internal architecture of self-compassion and self-care is equally, if not more, crucial for long-term recovery and relapse prevention. Think of it this way: your support network is like a sturdy bridge helping you cross a ravine; self-compassion and self-care are the strong foundations that ensure the bridge remains stable and capable of withstanding the forces of stress and adversity.

Self-compassion, in essence, is treating yourself with the same kindness, understanding, and concern you would offer a dear friend struggling with similar challenges. It's acknowledging your suffering without judgment, recognizing that you are not alone in your experience, and reminding yourself that you deserve kindness and compassion, even amidst imperfection. This is particularly vital after trauma, where self-criticism and self-blame are often deeply ingrained. Learning to replace self-criticism with self-compassion is a transformative process that fosters emotional resilience. It's about recognizing your inherent worthiness, regardless of past experiences or perceived failures.

Self-care, on the other hand, is the practical manifestation of self-compassion. It encompasses the conscious choices you make to nurture your physical, emotional, and mental well-being. It's not about indulging in fleeting pleasures or escaping your difficulties; it's about proactively engaging in activities that replenish your resources and enhance your capacity to cope with stress. This requires a profound understanding of your individual needs and preferences, a process of self-discovery that unfolds gradually as you navigate your healing journey. What constitutes self-care for one individual might be entirely different for another. There is no one-size-fits-all approach.

Consider creating a personalized self-care checklist, a living document that evolves alongside your healing journey. This checklist should include both regular practices and those you engage in during times of increased stress or vulnerability. Here are some examples to inspire your own personalized checklist:

Physical Self-Care: This focuses on the needs of your body. This might include:

Regular exercise: Find an activity you enjoy, whether it's yoga, swimming, walking, dancing, or something else entirely. The goal is to move your body regularly, even if it's just for a short period each day. The benefits extend beyond physical fitness, impacting mood regulation and stress reduction.

Nourishing diet: Focus on consuming whole, unprocessed foods that provide your body with the nutrients it needs to function optimally. This doesn't mean strict dieting; it's about making conscious choices to support your well-being. Pay attention to how different foods affect your energy levels and mood.

Adequate sleep: Aim for 7-9 hours of quality sleep each night. Establish a consistent sleep schedule, create a relaxing bedtime routine, and optimize your sleep environment to enhance sleep quality.

Mindful movement: Incorporate practices like yoga, tai chi, or qigong, which emphasize gentle movement, breathwork, and mindfulness, fostering a connection between mind and body.

Hydration: Ensure you are drinking enough water throughout the day. Dehydration can exacerbate stress and fatigue.

Regular medical check-ups: Maintain regular visits to your doctor and dentist for preventative care and address any physical health concerns promptly.

Emotional Self-Care: This involves nurturing your emotional landscape. This might include:

Journaling: Regularly writing down your thoughts and feelings can be a powerful tool for processing emotions and gaining self-awareness.

Mindfulness practices: Incorporating mindfulness meditation, even for just a few minutes each day, can significantly improve emotional regulation and reduce stress. Mindfulness involves paying attention to the present moment without judgment, allowing you to observe your thoughts and feelings without getting carried away by them.

Spending time in nature: Connecting with nature has been shown to reduce stress and improve mood. Spending time outdoors, whether it's a walk in the park or a hike in the mountains, can be incredibly restorative.

Creative expression: Engage in activities that allow you to express yourself creatively, such as painting, drawing, writing, music, or dancing.

Emotional processing: Actively processing your emotions through journaling, therapy, or other means is crucial. Don't bottle up your feelings; allow yourself to feel them fully and healthily.

Setting boundaries: Learning to set healthy boundaries with others is essential for protecting your emotional well-being. This might involve saying "no" to requests that drain your energy or compromise your values.

Mental Self-Care: This focuses on your cognitive well-being. This might include:

Cognitive restructuring: Identifying and challenging negative or unhelpful thought patterns is essential for improving mental well-being. A therapist can provide guidance on this process.

Learning new skills: Engage in activities that stimulate your mind and expand your knowledge and skills. This could involve taking a class, learning a new language, or pursuing a hobby.

Reading: Engaging with literature can provide comfort, inspiration, and new perspectives.

Limiting exposure to negativity: Reduce your exposure to negative news, social media, or other sources of negativity that might exacerbate stress.

Positive affirmations: Regularly repeating positive affirmations can help shift your mindset and improve self-esteem.

Mindful breathing techniques: Practicing controlled breathing techniques, such as diaphragmatic breathing, can help calm your nervous system and reduce anxiety.

Spiritual Self-Care: This involves nurturing your connection to something larger than yourself. This might include:

Meditation and prayer: Engaging in spiritual practices such as meditation or prayer can foster a sense of peace, purpose, and connection.

Spending time in nature: Many people find a deep connection to nature as a form of spiritual renewal.

Connecting with community: Participating in religious or spiritual communities can offer support, belonging, and a sense of purpose.

Acts of service: Helping others can foster a sense of meaning and purpose.

Mindfulness and gratitude practices: Practicing gratitude and appreciating the positive aspects of life can improve overall well-being and perspective.

It is essential to remember that these are simply suggestions; your self-care checklist should be tailored to your specific needs and preferences. Experiment with different practices to see what works best for you. Some days, you might prioritize physical self-care, while on other days, emotional or mental self-care might be paramount. The key is consistency and self-awareness. Regularly review and adjust your checklist as your needs evolve.

Self-compassion and self-care are not luxuries; they are essential components of trauma recovery and relapse prevention. By consistently nurturing your physical, emotional, and mental well-being, you are building the foundation for a stronger, more resilient self, capable of navigating the challenges that inevitably arise. Remember, your healing journey is a marathon, not a sprint. Be patient with yourself, celebrate your progress, and never hesitate to seek support when you need it. The investment you make in yourself through self-compassion and self-care will yield immeasurable rewards. It's about building a life that supports your well-being, not merely surviving, but thriving. The resilience you cultivate will not only help you overcome challenges but will also empower you to live a more fulfilling and meaningful life.

Celebrating milestones, no matter how small, is crucial for sustaining momentum in the healing process. Trauma recovery is a marathon, not a sprint, and acknowledging your progress along the way is vital for maintaining motivation and preventing relapse. It's easy to get caught up in the challenges and setbacks, often overlooking the significant strides you've made. This section focuses on actively recognizing and celebrating these achievements, however seemingly insignificant they may appear.

The human brain is wired to focus on threats and potential dangers. This is a survival mechanism that served our ancestors well, but in the context of healing, this focus can become a hindrance. It can lead to a constant hypervigilance for potential relapse, overshadowing the positive progress you've made. Therefore, intentionally shifting your attention to celebrate achievements helps rebalance this inherent bias, fostering a more optimistic and hopeful outlook.

Begin by identifying specific achievements, no matter how small. Did you complete a therapy session? Did you successfully navigate a challenging social interaction? Did you maintain your self-care routine for a week? Each of these represents a step forward on your healing journey. Keep a journal dedicated to recording these wins – a "success log" as it were. This log isn't about self-congratulation; it's about documenting your progress and building a tangible record of your resilience. Write down the specific action, the date, and a brief reflection on how it made you feel. This conscious act of documentation helps solidify your accomplishments in your mind and counteracts the tendency to minimize or dismiss them.

The act of writing itself is therapeutic. The process of articulating your achievements, however minor, allows you to reflect upon the effort involved and the positive impact it has had on your well-being. This reflection can enhance self-awareness, fostering a deeper understanding of your strengths and resilience. It provides an opportunity to acknowledge your efforts, recognize your growth, and reinforce your commitment to healing.

Beyond journaling, consider other ways to acknowledge your milestones. This might involve a small reward, a mindful moment of appreciation, or sharing your success with a trusted friend, family member, or therapist. The reward shouldn't be something that undermines your progress, like overindulging in unhealthy foods or substances. Instead, choose something that supports your self-care, such as taking a long bath, reading a good book, or enjoying a peaceful walk in nature.

Sharing your accomplishments with your support network can also significantly impact your well-being. This provides an opportunity to receive validation and encouragement, fostering a sense of community and shared experience. Moreover, the very act of verbalizing your progress can help reinforce its significance in your mind, strengthening your sense of self-efficacy and boosting your confidence in your ability to continue healing. Remember to be specific when you share your progress. Instead of saying "I'm doing better," say "I've been consistently practicing mindfulness for a week now, and it has helped me manage my anxiety more effectively." Specificity strengthens the impact of your words and helps those around you understand the depth of your achievements.

Visual reminders can also be helpful. Create a vision board representing your goals and progress. Include images and affirmations that reflect your hopes for the future, as well as tangible evidence of your achievements so far. This visual representation serves as a constant source of motivation and reinforcement, reminding you of how far you've come and encouraging you to continue moving forward. You could also utilize a gratitude journal, specifically focusing on the progress you've made. Write down three things you're grateful for each day, including accomplishments big and small. This shifts your focus to positivity and builds a sense of appreciation for the journey.

It's important to avoid comparing your journey to others'. Remember that healing is a deeply personal and individualized process. There is no "right" pace or timeline. Your journey is unique, and celebrating your own milestones, according to your own pace and personal benchmarks, is far more effective than striving to meet external expectations.

Incorporate self-compassion into your celebrations. Acknowledge that setbacks will occur. Don't allow a setback to derail your progress; view it as a temporary obstacle, a learning opportunity that helps you refine your approach. When you encounter a setback, review your success log, reminding yourself of all you have already achieved. This perspective can significantly mitigate feelings of discouragement and maintain your motivation.

Maintain regular communication with your therapist or support network. Discuss your progress, your challenges, and your celebrations. This provides valuable external validation and perspective, helping you maintain a balanced perspective on your journey. A support system can offer encouragement during challenging times, and actively celebrate your achievements. Their acknowledgment of your progress reinforces the validity of your efforts.

Celebrating milestones isn't about boasting or self-aggrandizement. It's a strategy for self-care, designed to counter the negative self-talk and hyper-focus on challenges that can hinder recovery. By actively acknowledging your achievements, you reinforce positive self-perception, cultivate resilience, and reduce the risk of relapse. Remember to be kind to yourself throughout this process. Your healing journey is a testament to your strength and perseverance, and it deserves to be acknowledged and celebrated at every stage. Consider it an ongoing process of self-discovery and empowerment. Every small step forward, every challenge overcome, is a significant victory that contributes to building a more resilient and fulfilling life.

The process of healing from trauma is often viewed as a struggle to reach a specific endpoint, a return to a presumed "normal" state of well-being. This model, however, can be quite limiting. It implies a sense of finality and completion that often doesn't reflect the ongoing nature of self-discovery and personal growth. Embracing the concept of ongoing growth is vital for sustainable recovery. Healing is not a destination, it's a journey, a continuous process of self-discovery and development.

Rather than focusing on achieving a state of "being healed," consider your recovery as a journey of becoming. This reframing broadens your perspective, moving beyond the confines of reaching a specific milestone and embracing ongoing growth and adaptation. The challenges you encounter along the way become opportunities for learning and deepening your self-understanding, enabling you to adapt and evolve as you navigate the complexities of life.

Celebrate the small victories. Acknowledge that you are resilient, capable, and resourceful. The strength you've demonstrated in facing your trauma is a testament to your innate capacity for healing and self-growth. By actively celebrating your progress, you cultivate a positive feedback loop that reinforces your efforts and sustains your motivation. This creates a foundation for long-term recovery and allows you to confidently embrace the ever-evolving nature of your healing journey. The ongoing process of celebrating your achievements contributes to a sense of agency and empowerment, bolstering your resilience and fostering a deeper appreciation for the strengths and capabilities you develop along the way.

Chapter 10: Living a Fulfilling Life

Building a life of fulfillment necessitates a deep understanding of oneself, and a crucial aspect of this self-awareness involves identifying and prioritizing your core values. These values aren't merely abstract ideals; they are the fundamental beliefs and principles that guide your decisions, shape your behaviors, and ultimately define what truly matters to you. They form the bedrock upon which you build your life, influencing your relationships, career choices, and overall sense of well-being. Without a clear understanding of your values, you risk drifting through life, making choices that ultimately leave you feeling unfulfilled and disconnected from your authentic self.

The process of identifying your values is a deeply personal and introspective one. There's no right or wrong answer; the key is to uncover what resonates most authentically with you. Begin by considering different aspects of your life. Think about moments when you felt a profound sense of joy, satisfaction, or purpose. What were you doing? What qualities or characteristics were present in those experiences? These moments often provide valuable clues to your underlying values.

For example, if you find immense satisfaction in volunteering at a local animal shelter, it might suggest that compassion, empathy, and service to others are among your core values. If you derive deep fulfillment from mastering a new skill, it might indicate that personal growth, competence, and achievement are important to you. If you consistently prioritize spending quality time with loved ones, this points to the importance of relationships, connection, and intimacy in your life.

To facilitate this reflection, consider using various exercises designed to illuminate your values. One effective method is to create a list of words or phrases that represent qualities you admire in yourself and others. These could include words like honesty, creativity, kindness, courage, independence, or perseverance. Once you have a substantial list, review it carefully and identify the words or phrases that resonate most strongly with you. These are likely to be closely aligned with your core values.

Another valuable exercise involves recalling specific moments in your life when you felt most alive and engaged. These moments might be related to significant achievements, overcoming challenges, or forming meaningful connections. Analyze these experiences, considering what aspects made them so fulfilling. What values were present or reinforced during these experiences? This retrospective analysis can provide significant insights into your underlying value system.

Beyond these individual exercises, consider engaging in more structured reflection. A values clarification exercise, often employed in therapy or self-help contexts, involves ranking a series of values in order of importance to you. This structured approach helps to articulate your values explicitly, facilitating a deeper understanding of their relative significance in your life. These values might include things like family, freedom, security, health, creativity, or spirituality. The process of ranking them, however, forces you to consciously consider the trade-offs involved in prioritizing some values over others.

Once you have identified your core values, the next step is to examine how your current life aligns with them. Are your daily actions, choices, and commitments reflecting these values? If there's a significant mismatch, you might find yourself experiencing feelings of dissatisfaction, frustration, or a general sense of being "off track." This mismatch is a strong indicator that you may need to make changes in your life to better align with your authentic self.

This process of alignment doesn't necessarily mean drastically altering your entire life overnight. It's often a gradual process of making small, incremental changes that bring your daily life into greater harmony with your values. This could involve making conscious choices to prioritize activities that resonate with your values, such as spending more time with loved ones, engaging in creative pursuits, or volunteering in your community. It might also involve setting boundaries to protect your time and energy from activities that drain you or conflict with your values.

For instance, if you value family connection but find yourself consistently overwhelmed by work, you might need to re-evaluate your workload, delegate responsibilities, or set clear boundaries between work and family time. If you value personal growth but find yourself stagnant in your current career, you might need to seek out opportunities for professional development or consider a career change. The key is to actively seek out ways to incorporate your values into your daily routines and decision-making processes.

The process of defining and prioritizing your values is an ongoing one. As you grow and evolve, your values may shift and evolve as well. This is a natural part of the human experience, and it's important to be open to this possibility. Regularly revisit your values, reflecting on how they align with your current life and making adjustments as needed. Consider this a continuous process of self-discovery and refinement, leading to a deeper understanding of yourself and your place in the world.

Furthermore, understanding your values is crucial not just for personal fulfillment, but also for navigating life's inevitable challenges. When faced with difficult decisions, your values provide a compass to guide you towards choices that are in alignment with your deepest beliefs and priorities. This can provide a sense of clarity and purpose, even amid uncertainty and stress. By basing your decisions on your core values, you create a sense of integrity and authenticity, fostering a stronger sense of self-worth and resilience.

The journey of defining your values and priorities is not a one-time event, but a continuous process of self-discovery and refinement. It's about actively engaging with your inner world, paying attention to your gut feelings, and making conscious choices that reflect your deepest values. By aligning your life with what truly matters to you, you create a foundation for a life filled with purpose, meaning, and lasting fulfillment. It's a journey of self-awareness, self-acceptance, and ultimately, self-creation. Embrace the process, allow for adjustments along the way, and remember that the goal isn't perfection, but progress towards a life that is authentically yours.

Living a fulfilling life often hinges on the ability to manage stress and adversity effectively. While defining your values provides a strong internal compass, developing coping mechanisms for challenging situations is equally critical. Consider your past experiences with stress. What strategies worked well for you? What approaches proved less effective? Understanding your personal strengths and weaknesses in stress management is the first step towards building a robust and sustainable approach.

Consider incorporating mindfulness practices into your daily routine. Mindfulness techniques such as meditation, deep breathing exercises, and mindful movement can help you cultivate a greater awareness of your thoughts, feelings, and bodily sensations. This heightened awareness enables you to identify and respond to stress more effectively, reducing the likelihood of overwhelming reactions. Regular practice of mindfulness can also cultivate emotional regulation skills, allowing you to approach challenging situations with greater calm and composure.

In addition to mindfulness, consider exploring other stress management techniques, such as cognitive behavioral therapy (CBT), which teaches you to identify and challenge negative thought patterns that contribute to stress and anxiety. Furthermore, somatic practices, such as yoga or tai chi, can help you connect with your body and release physical tension associated with stress. These approaches are complementary, offering a holistic approach to stress management, supporting emotional regulation, and enhancing your overall resilience.

Remember, the pursuit of a fulfilling life is an ongoing journey, not a destination. There will be moments of challenge and setback, but by continually refining your self-awareness, clarifying your values, and building robust coping mechanisms, you can create a life that is authentic, meaningful, and deeply fulfilling. The process itself is a journey of self-discovery and growth, enriching your life in ways you might not anticipate. Embrace the journey, celebrate your progress, and trust in your inherent capacity for growth and resilience.

Having established a strong foundation of self-awareness and a clear understanding of your core values, the next crucial step in crafting a fulfilling life involves setting meaningful goals. These goals aren't arbitrary aspirations; rather, they are carefully constructed milestones that align directly with your values, providing direction and purpose on your journey. The process of goal-setting, when approached thoughtfully, becomes a powerful tool for personal growth and the achievement of lasting fulfillment.

Unlike fleeting resolutions or impulsive desires, meaningful goals are deeply rooted in your intrinsic motivations. They stem from a genuine desire to live a life congruent with your values, not simply to meet external expectations or chase fleeting trends. This intrinsic connection fuels your commitment and provides resilience when faced with inevitable challenges. The process of setting these goals is itself an exercise in self-discovery, prompting further reflection on your priorities and aspirations.

To begin, consider your core values once more. How can you translate these abstract principles into tangible, achievable goals? If connection and intimacy are paramount, a meaningful goal might involve strengthening existing relationships or cultivating new ones. This could entail scheduling regular quality time with loved ones, engaging in shared activities, or actively nurturing emotional intimacy through open communication. It's not just about quantity of time spent, but the quality of interaction and the depth of connection fostered.

If personal growth is a core value, consider setting goals related to skill development, learning new things, or expanding your knowledge base. This might involve enrolling in a course, pursuing a hobby, reading widely, or seeking out mentorship opportunities. The emphasis should be on continuous learning and expansion of your capabilities, reflecting your commitment to self-improvement and personal evolution. Remember to choose areas of learning that genuinely excite you, aligning your goals with your passions and interests. Avoid setting goals solely based on external pressures or perceived societal expectations.

Suppose creativity and self-expression are central to your values. Then your goals might involve engaging in artistic pursuits, writing, music, or any other creative endeavor that allows you to express yourself authentically. This could involve dedicating specific time slots for creative work, joining a creative community, or seeking feedback on your creations to help you refine your skills and explore new avenues of expression. The goal here is not necessarily to achieve mastery or external validation, but to engage in the process of creation itself, fostering self-discovery and fulfilling your creative potential.

For those who value physical health and well-being, setting meaningful goals might involve adopting healthier lifestyle habits, such as regular exercise, mindful eating, or prioritizing adequate sleep. This could entail establishing a consistent exercise routine, planning nutritious meals, or creating a relaxing bedtime routine. Remember, these goals should be sustainable and tailored to your individual circumstances and preferences. Avoid setting unrealistic expectations that are likely to lead to discouragement and abandonment. Focus on gradual, incremental progress rather than striving for perfection overnight.

When setting these goals, it's vital to employ the SMART framework: Specific, Measurable, Achievable, Relevant, and Time-bound. A vague goal, such as "improve my health," is far less effective than a specific, measurable one, such as "walk for 30 minutes, three times a week, for the next three months." This level of specificity provides clarity and allows you to track your progress, fostering a sense of accomplishment and reinforcing your commitment. Ensure that your goals are relevant to your values and are attainable within a realistic timeframe. Avoid setting goals that are overly ambitious or overwhelming, as this can lead to frustration and decreased motivation.

Consider the potential obstacles that might hinder your progress toward your goals. Identify these challenges proactively and develop strategies to overcome them. If a lack of time is a barrier, explore ways to optimize your schedule, delegate tasks, or eliminate time-wasting activities. If a lack of resources poses a problem, explore alternative solutions, such as seeking financial assistance, utilizing community resources, or finding creative ways to work within your constraints. This proactive approach helps to build resilience and reinforces your commitment to achieving your goals.

Furthermore, it's crucial to integrate your goals into your daily routine. Schedule dedicated time for pursuing your goals, ensuring that they are not relegated to the periphery of your life. Make them a non-negotiable part of your day, just like other essential commitments. Treat your goal pursuit with the same level of respect and seriousness as you would any important appointment or deadline. This approach underscores the importance of your goals and reinforces your commitment to achieving them.

Regularly review your progress toward your goals and make adjustments as needed. Life is dynamic and unexpected events may arise, requiring adjustments to your plans. Don't be discouraged by setbacks or temporary deviations from your path. View these as opportunities for learning and refinement, recalibrating your approach and strengthening your resolve. The process of goal-setting is not linear; it's an iterative process of refinement and adaptation, enabling you to grow and evolve along the way.

Celebrate your achievements along the way. Acknowledge your successes, no matter how small. This positive reinforcement reinforces your commitment and motivates you to continue striving toward your goals. Recognize and appreciate the effort you've invested, celebrating your progress and fostering a sense of accomplishment. This positive self-talk helps to maintain momentum and build resilience when facing setbacks.

Remember, the ultimate aim is not merely to achieve your goals, but to cultivate a sense of purpose, meaning, and fulfillment throughout the process. Your goals should contribute to a life that aligns with your values and enriches your overall well-being. Setting meaningful goals is not just about achieving specific outcomes; it's about cultivating a deeper sense of self-awareness, purpose, and personal growth. It's about creating a life that truly reflects your values and aspirations, leading to a profound sense of fulfillment and satisfaction. Embrace the journey, celebrate your progress, and remember that the pursuit of a fulfilling life is a continuous process of growth and self-discovery. Trust in your ability to navigate challenges, adapt to changes, and create a life that resonates with your authentic self.

Cultivating gratitude is not merely a fleeting sentiment; it's a powerful practice that can profoundly reshape our perception of life and enhance our overall well-being. While the challenges and stressors of daily life often dominate our attention, consciously focusing on what we appreciate fosters a shift in perspective, allowing us to recognize the abundance present even amidst adversity. This isn't about ignoring hardship or pretending negativity doesn't exist; rather, it's about creating a balance – acknowledging the difficult while simultaneously appreciating the positive elements that often go unnoticed.

The benefits of gratitude extend far beyond a simple feeling of happiness. Studies consistently demonstrate a strong correlation between gratitude and improved mental health. Individuals who regularly practice gratitude tend to experience lower levels of stress, anxiety, and depression. This is because gratitude acts as an antidote to negativity bias, the tendency to focus more on negative experiences than positive ones. By consciously shifting our attention towards what we're grateful for, we actively counteract this bias and cultivate a more optimistic outlook.

Furthermore, gratitude enhances our relationships. Expressing gratitude to others strengthens bonds and fosters a sense of connection and belonging. When we express appreciation, we not only make the recipient feel valued, but we also experience a boost in our own well-being. This reciprocal effect creates a positive feedback loop, strengthening relationships and enriching our social lives. This is particularly important in the context of trauma recovery, where rebuilding trust and connection are crucial for healing. Expressing gratitude can serve as a powerful tool for reconnecting with others and fostering a sense of safety and support.

The practice of gratitude isn't about ignoring problems or minimizing challenges. Instead, it's about cultivating a more balanced perspective, allowing us to appreciate the good in life even amidst difficulties. This perspective shift doesn't diminish the significance of challenges; it simply adds another layer to our understanding – a recognition of the resilience and strength we've developed in overcoming adversity, the support we've received from others, and the positive aspects of our lives that persist despite hardship.

Several practical techniques can help cultivate and deepen your practice of gratitude. One of the most effective methods is keeping a gratitude journal. This simple yet powerful tool involves regularly writing down things you're grateful for. This could be anything from the simple pleasure of a warm cup of coffee to a significant accomplishment, a supportive friendship, or the beauty of nature. The act of writing helps solidify the feeling of gratitude, making it more tangible and lasting. It also serves as a record of your progress, providing tangible evidence of the positive aspects in your life, which can be particularly valuable during times of stress or challenge. Consider starting small, with just three entries a day, and gradually increasing as you become more comfortable with the practice.

The frequency of journaling is crucial; consistency is key. Daily entries are ideal, but even a few times a week can make a significant difference. The key is to establish a routine that fits seamlessly into your daily life. You might choose to journal first thing in the morning to set a positive tone for the day, or before bed to reflect on the day's blessings. Alternatively, you might find it more helpful to dedicate a specific time slot each day, creating a dedicated space and time for this reflective practice. Experiment with different times and approaches until you discover a rhythm that aligns with your lifestyle and preferences.

Beyond journaling, mindful reflection can also be a powerful tool for cultivating gratitude. This involves taking a few moments each day to consciously focus on aspects of your life that you appreciate. This might be during a quiet moment in nature, while meditating, or simply while sipping your morning tea. Close your eyes, breathe deeply, and allow yourself to become fully present in the moment. Then, bring your attention to the things you feel grateful for – the warmth of the sun on your skin, the taste of your tea, the supportive presence of a loved one. Allow yourself to feel the emotion of gratitude deeply, immersing yourself fully in the experience. The more senses you can engage in this practice, the richer and more profound the experience will be.

Another effective technique involves expressing gratitude to others. A simple "thank you" can go a long way in fostering positive connections and strengthening relationships. Consider writing thank-you notes to people who have impacted your life positively, expressing your sincere appreciation for their support and kindness. The act of writing these notes not only benefits the recipient but also deepens your own feelings of gratitude. It allows you to reflect on the positive impact others have had on your life, reinforcing the importance of connection and support in your journey. This is a particularly powerful technique in the context of trauma recovery, as it can help you reconnect with supportive figures and rebuild trust.

Similarly, expressing gratitude for yourself is equally important. Acknowledge your own efforts, resilience, and accomplishments, no matter how small. Often, we're quick to criticize ourselves but slow to recognize our strengths and successes. Make a conscious effort to celebrate your achievements, recognizing the effort and dedication you've invested in overcoming challenges. This self-compassion is crucial for building self-esteem and fostering a sense of self-worth. This is especially significant after experiencing trauma, where self-criticism and feelings of inadequacy can be prevalent.

Beyond these structured practices, incorporating gratitude into everyday life can also be significantly impactful. This involves consciously pausing to appreciate everyday moments, noticing the small joys and blessings that often go unnoticed. This could include appreciating the beauty of a sunrise, the comfort of a warm blanket, or the laughter of a child. These seemingly insignificant moments, when viewed through the lens of gratitude, can become sources of significant joy and fulfillment. Cultivating this awareness and attentiveness enhances the richness and depth of everyday experiences.

Incorporating gratitude into your daily routine, however you choose to do so, is a profound act of self-care. It is a proactive approach to enhance your emotional well-being, fostering resilience and cultivating a more positive outlook. Remember that the practice of gratitude is not a quick fix, but rather a journey of cultivating appreciation and awareness. The more consistent your practice, the more profound its impact on your overall well-being. Embrace the process, allowing yourself to explore different techniques and find the approaches that resonate most deeply with you.

The journey of cultivating gratitude is a personal one. Experiment with different methods, find what works best for you, and adapt your practice as needed. Consistency is key, but flexibility is equally important. Allow yourself to explore different approaches to find what resonates with you. Don't be discouraged if you miss a day or two – simply acknowledge it, and gently return to your practice. Remember that the goal isn't perfection, but progress. The process itself, the conscious effort to focus on what you appreciate, is a significant step towards fostering a more fulfilling and resilient life. The act of cultivating gratitude is not just about acknowledging the positive; it's about actively choosing to focus on it, shaping our perspective and ultimately enriching our experience of life. This consistent focus not only improves our emotional well-being, but it also strengthens our sense of purpose and connection to the world around us. By shifting our attention to the positive aspects of our lives, we create a more fertile ground for growth, resilience, and sustained well-being. This is especially true after traumatic experiences, where shifting the focus to gratitude can play a vital role in healing and creating a path towards a more fulfilling future.

Embracing imperfection is not about lowering our standards; it's about shifting our perspective on what constitutes success and fulfillment. The relentless pursuit of perfection often fuels a cycle of self-criticism and dissatisfaction. We become hyper-focused on our flaws, magnifying minor imperfections into major shortcomings. This can lead to feelings of inadequacy, anxiety, and even depression, hindering our ability to appreciate our strengths and accomplishments. Instead of striving for an unattainable ideal, we must learn to accept ourselves, flaws and all. This acceptance doesn't mean complacency; it means acknowledging our imperfections while still striving for growth and improvement. It's about recognizing that our worth is not contingent on achieving flawless execution in every aspect of our lives.

Self-compassion, a cornerstone of self-acceptance, involves treating ourselves with the same kindness and understanding we would offer a close friend struggling with similar challenges. It requires recognizing that everyone makes mistakes, experiences setbacks, and falls short of their aspirations at times. Instead of harshly judging ourselves for our imperfections, we can offer ourselves empathy, forgiveness, and encouragement. This involves acknowledging our suffering, recognizing that we are not alone in our struggles, and reminding ourselves that we are worthy of kindness and compassion.

The journey toward self-acceptance is often gradual and requires conscious effort. It involves challenging negative self-talk, reframing our thoughts, and cultivating a more positive self-image. This can be achieved through various techniques, such as mindfulness meditation, cognitive behavioral therapy (CBT), and journaling. Mindfulness encourages us to observe our thoughts and feelings without judgment, allowing us to become more aware of our self-critical tendencies. CBT provides tools to identify and challenge negative thought patterns, replacing them with more realistic and balanced perspectives. Journaling offers a space to explore our thoughts and emotions, gain self-awareness, and track our progress on the path to self-acceptance.

One effective journaling exercise is to identify three things you appreciate about yourself each day. These could be small things, such as your kindness to a stranger, your perseverance in facing a challenge, or your ability to find joy in simple pleasures. It's crucial to focus on the positive aspects of yourself, celebrating your strengths and acknowledging your efforts. This practice shifts the focus away from perceived imperfections and cultivates a more balanced and positive self-image.

Another beneficial practice is to actively challenge negative self-talk. When you notice yourself engaging in self-criticism, pause and ask yourself: "Would I say this to a friend?" If the answer is no, then reframe the statement into something more compassionate and supportive. For example, instead of thinking, "I'm such a failure," try "I made a mistake, but I can learn from it and do better next time." This simple shift in perspective can significantly impact your self-perception and emotional well-being. This reframing is crucial after experiencing trauma, as self-criticism and self-blame are common reactions.

Self-acceptance also involves setting realistic expectations. It's important to acknowledge that we are multifaceted individuals with diverse strengths and weaknesses. We shouldn't strive for perfection in every area of our lives. Instead, we should focus on setting attainable goals and celebrating our progress, no matter how small. This process involves identifying areas where we want to grow and develop, while accepting and embracing our limitations. This is particularly important after experiencing trauma; setting manageable goals can prevent overwhelm and promote a sense of accomplishment.

Embracing imperfection involves actively choosing to focus on our strengths rather than dwelling on our weaknesses. This requires self-reflection and honest assessment of our skills and abilities. Identify areas where you excel, and actively seek opportunities to utilize these strengths. This can boost your self-confidence and reinforce your belief in your capabilities. It's a powerful way to counter the negative self-talk and self-doubt that often accompanies a focus on imperfections.

Furthermore, cultivating self-compassion involves acknowledging our humanness. We all make mistakes; it's part of being human. Learning to forgive ourselves for our imperfections is crucial for our emotional well-being. Holding onto past mistakes and self-criticism only perpetuates feelings of guilt and shame. Forgiving ourselves allows us to move forward, learn from our experiences, and focus on creating a more fulfilling future. This process can be especially challenging after trauma, where self-blame and guilt can be pervasive.

Self-acceptance is not a destination but a continuous process of self-discovery and growth. It requires consistent effort, self-reflection, and a commitment to cultivating self-compassion. There will be times when we slip back into self-critical patterns, and that's okay. The key is to acknowledge these setbacks, gently redirect our thoughts, and continue to practice self-acceptance. The journey towards self-acceptance is a testament to our resilience and our commitment to our own well-being.

The benefits of self-acceptance extend far beyond increased self-esteem and reduced self-criticism. It significantly impacts our relationships, our ability to cope with stress, and our overall life satisfaction. When we accept ourselves, we're better equipped to build healthy relationships based on authenticity and mutual respect. We're less likely to seek validation from external sources, and more comfortable expressing our true selves.

Similarly, self-acceptance enhances our resilience to stress. When confronted with challenges, we're better able to cope with setbacks without succumbing to self-doubt or despair. We can approach challenges with a more balanced perspective, acknowledging our imperfections while maintaining confidence in our ability to overcome obstacles. This resilience is crucial, especially in the aftermath of trauma, where the ability to cope with stress and adversity is paramount.

Finally, self-acceptance fosters a sense of overall life satisfaction. When we accept ourselves, we are better able to appreciate the positive aspects of our lives and enjoy the journey. We're less likely to be consumed by the pursuit of an unattainable ideal and more likely to find fulfillment in the present moment. This shift in perspective creates space for gratitude, joy, and a deeper appreciation for the richness and complexity of life. This perspective is essential for creating a truly fulfilling life, especially after trauma, where rebuilding a sense of purpose and joy is a crucial part of the healing process.

In conclusion, embracing imperfection and self-acceptance is a vital step towards living a fulfilling life. It requires consistent effort, self-compassion, and a willingness to challenge our negative self-talk. The journey is not always easy, but the rewards—enhanced self-esteem, resilience, and life satisfaction—are immeasurable. By cultivating self-acceptance, we create a foundation for growth, healing, and a more fulfilling existence. This journey, particularly after trauma, represents a profound act of self-care and a crucial step toward building a brighter and more resilient future. The act of accepting our imperfections is not about settling for less; it's about freeing ourselves from the burden of an unrealistic ideal, allowing us to embrace our true selves and live authentically. It is a powerful act of self-love and a crucial ingredient in building a truly fulfilling and meaningful life. This self-acceptance is not a passive resignation to our flaws; rather, it's an active choice to embrace our whole selves—strengths and weaknesses—as integral parts of who we are. This acceptance allows us to move beyond self-criticism and cultivate a more compassionate and understanding relationship with ourselves, which is essential for navigating the complexities of life and building a future filled with purpose, joy, and resilience.

Building a life imbued with purpose and meaning is not a destination but a continuous journey of self-discovery and growth. It's a process of actively shaping our experiences, aligning our actions with our values, and cultivating a deep sense of connection to something larger than ourselves. This involves identifying our passions, exploring our talents, and setting goals that resonate with our deepest aspirations. It requires courage to step outside our comfort zones, embrace challenges, and learn from setbacks. The lessons learned in embracing imperfection and cultivating self-compassion provide a strong foundation for this journey.

One of the most crucial steps in creating a life of purpose is identifying our core values. These are the principles that guide our decisions and actions, shaping our sense of self and our interactions with the world. Take time for introspection. Reflect on the moments in your life when you felt most alive, most fulfilled. What were you doing? Who were you with? What qualities did you embody? These moments often reveal our underlying values. They might include things like creativity, connection, contribution, growth, learning, or integrity. Once identified, these values act as a compass, guiding us toward choices that are aligned with our true selves.

Once you've identified your core values, consider how they are currently reflected in your life. Are you living in alignment with them? Or are there areas where you feel a disconnect? This honest self-assessment is crucial. It may reveal areas where you need to make changes, adjustments to your lifestyle, career, or relationships. This process might feel uncomfortable initially, requiring a willingness to confront ingrained patterns and potentially challenging choices.

Setting meaningful goals is another essential component of building a life of purpose. These goals should align with your values and aspirations.

They should be challenging yet attainable, inspiring you to grow and develop while remaining grounded in reality. Avoid setting overly ambitious goals that might lead to feelings of overwhelm and frustration. Instead, focus on small, manageable steps that build momentum and contribute to your long-term vision. Regularly review and adjust your goals as needed, adapting to changing circumstances and new insights. Remember, the journey is as important as the destination. Celebrate your progress along the way, acknowledging your achievements, no matter how small.

Cultivating meaningful relationships is crucial for a fulfilling life. These relationships provide support, encouragement, and a sense of belonging. Nurture your connections with loved ones, investing time and energy in building strong, healthy relationships. Seek out new connections with people who share your values and interests. These relationships can offer diverse perspectives, enriching your life and broadening your understanding of the world. Remember that healthy relationships are reciprocal, requiring effort, compromise, and mutual respect.

Contributing to something larger than ourselves fosters a sense of purpose and meaning. This could involve volunteering for a cause you care about, mentoring others, or simply acts of kindness towards strangers. The act of giving back can provide a profound sense of fulfillment, connecting us to something greater than our individual selves. Consider your passions and skills and identify ways to utilize them in service to others. This contribution could involve formal volunteering or simply integrating acts of kindness into your daily life.

Engaging in activities that bring you joy and fulfillment is essential for maintaining a sense of well-being. These could be hobbies, creative pursuits, or simply spending time in nature. Make time for these activities, prioritizing them in your schedule, even if it means sacrificing other less important tasks. These activities serve as a source of rejuvenation and inspiration, fueling your energy and enthusiasm for life. Remember that self-care is not selfish; it's an essential component of a healthy and balanced life.

Mindfulness and somatic practices, discussed in previous chapters, remain vital tools in building a life of purpose. Mindfulness cultivates present moment awareness, helping us to appreciate the richness and complexity of our experiences. Somatic practices connect us to our bodies, enhancing our self-awareness and resilience. By integrating these practices into our daily lives, we can develop a deeper understanding of ourselves and our place in the world. This self-awareness becomes a powerful resource in navigating challenges and making choices aligned with our values.

The journey toward a life of purpose is not always linear. There will be setbacks, obstacles, and moments of doubt. Embrace these challenges as opportunities for growth and learning. Reflect on your experiences, identifying lessons learned and adjusting your course as needed. Remember the resilience you have developed through previous struggles, drawing on your strengths and resources.

Furthermore, cultivating gratitude is a powerful tool in enhancing our sense of fulfillment. Regularly reflecting on the positive aspects of our lives—our relationships, our health, our accomplishments—can shift our perspective, promoting a sense of appreciation and contentment.

Keeping a gratitude journal can be a helpful tool, prompting us to focus on the good in our lives.

In conclusion, creating a life of purpose and meaning is a personal journey requiring self-reflection, goal setting, and a commitment to living in alignment with our values. It involves cultivating meaningful relationships, contributing to something larger than ourselves, engaging in activities that bring us joy, and utilizing mindfulness and somatic practices to enhance our self-awareness and resilience. Remember that the journey is ongoing, requiring adaptation and perseverance. Embrace the challenges, celebrate the victories, and cherish the journey itself. The process of building a fulfilling life is, in itself, a testament to our capacity for growth, resilience, and the enduring human spirit. This is a life built not on the avoidance of suffering, but on the courageous navigation of it, a life enriched by the lessons learned and the meaning we create along the way. It is a journey of constant evolution, refinement, and self-discovery, reflecting the dynamic and ever-changing nature of the human experience. It's a life lived with intention, purpose, and a deep appreciation for the precious gift of existence itself. And most importantly, it's a life lived authentically, truthfully, and in alignment with the unique and beautiful individual that you are.